Lust For Life

Sylvester McNutt III

© 2017 Sylvester McNutt III

All rights reserved. No part of this book may be reproduced or transmitted in any form or by any means, electronic or mechanical, including photocopying, recording, or by an information storage and retrieval system—except by a reviewer who may quote brief passages in a review to be printed in a magazine or newspaper—without permission in writing from the publisher.

ISBN-13: 978-0692920459
ISBN: 0692920455

The names in all of these stories, poems, and anecdotes have been changed to protect the identities of any person(s) real, exaggerated, or made up. *Lust For Life* and Sylvester McNutt III are not suggesting or promoting any lifestyle or choices in this book. This book is written as a true expression of art, of poetry, and of creativity. This book is written from the perspective and opinion of the creator, and he reserves the right, at any moment, to change his perception of anything presented. The author, the publisher, or person responsible for delivering you this text is not liable for any undesirable outcome.

Lust For Life

Sylvester McNutt III

All social media links, contact info, bio,

and speaking dates can be found at:

www.sylvestermcnutt.net

Few will have the greatness to bend history, itself, but each of us can work to change a small portion of events, and in the total of these acts will be written the history of each generation.

—Sen. Robert F. Kennedy
Cape Town, South 1966

Chapters

Lust For Life

The world we live in is mad, illogical, and insane. This is not a new observation. It's not sad; it's not anything to get too upset over. This is only something we should observe and react to. Wars have been fought for as far back as we can remember, with religions separating people and human beings buying into the separation to cause more suffering among us. We come into this world and think that we are coming into a world, instead of realizing that we are coming from it. We are taught to believe that our life is the most important one, that our goals are more important, and that savagery is simply the human way.

There have always been deception and people who try to hoard power and resources. There has always been a group of people who chase dominance to call themselves elitist—some for survival and others for ego and status. In America, our government is trillions of dollars in debt, we have no financial education, and our marriage rates decline even as obesity and disease increase. We have increasing access to information because this is the technology era, but we are less equipped to use common sense: reason, logic, awareness. There are still countries in the world that use slavery as a means to building wealth. There are still countries going to war over resources and imaginary landlines that create divisions.

We are told to go to school for the first twenty to twenty-five years of our life just to come out in debt, trapped in a system where nobody understands finances, and are then expected to get a job that can support us and our families that we desire to start. We live in a generation that is obsessed with creating a race war; I don't think it's everyone, but a lot of people have opinions and are trying to use the media to create tension. I've always seen myself as a human being, and somehow making a statement like that in this culture will get you attacked by one group or another. One group will be mad because the melanin in my skin tells me that I should have an unshakable pride in that melanin and that I should speak up for the rights of others who share my skin color because we have been oppressed. Simply saying that I don't identify with a race and that I am just human would cause conflict; in fact this is a trigger point for some people, and you're trying to decipher if I'm actually saying it or if I'm just using prose poetry to make a connection. We live in a world where assumptions are more important than facts, and jumping to conclusions is more important than being patient and doing the research. If I tell you that I've studied Buddhist ways, then you will have a perception of what I know based on what they teach, which isn't the case, or is it? If I tell you that I was raised Christian and that I reject the religion because of the millions of lives that have been lost in the name of religion, you might scoff at me. If I tell you that I was born on August 23 and you're into horoscopes, you'll have an entire breakdown of who I might be based on what some book has told you about who I am. We have a world of people who believe, without a shadow of doubt, that my birthday complexity controls my behaviors. These types of people will completely overrule the environment one grew up in, the neighborhood, potential traumatic childhood experiences, or ideologies that one does or does not accept. Because I'm a Virgo, you instantly box me into an expectation. Because of the melanin in my skin, you box me into an expectation of behavior that the media has shown you—not one that I have shown you through actual interaction but one that the media has given you. Is this wrong? I can't sit here and tell you that nor do I have the energy to do so, but it's not efficient. It's not the smartest process. It doesn't seem to be very open and thoughtful to the actual life that each human being has. To subjectively judge someone as you're getting to know him or her, without allowing the person complete space and reign to be his or her natural organic self, seems like an imposed prison for the person to live in. A prison of any kind seems to evoke hatred, conflict, depression, and sadness.

The earth has abundant blue waters that scour our entire sphere. Animals, plants, organisms, bacteria, and human beings all share this one ecosystem that essentially spawns millions of other kingdoms and ecosystems. Your ego tells you that this experience is about "I," and it might be, but what guides you, what probes your mind, and who challenges you to dig deep inside all of this to find your true bliss and peace? This book, if I write it well enough, should only help you and should only rattle your senses to your natural *Lust For Life*. I hear lots of people who make claims about how they want to change the world, introduce world peace, and stop diseases, and as noble as that sounds, it also sounds like a waste of time. Sounds harsh, eh? It might be, but we aren't here to judge the entire world. That's honestly not what this book is about. This book is about your quest, your curious journey, your mood swings, the jobs that build you up, love that feels like summer, and the memories that you forget but also the people that you do not. *Lust for Life* isn't about the moral and noble code of fixing the world. Let's start with the individual and focus on each inner world before we focus on the collective outer world. My mission, as the writer of this book, is to help you reconnect to your earth, to your curiosities, to your complexities, to lust, to love, to passion, and to purpose. With every book that I write, I have an underlying goal to help the reader let go or release something that is holding him or her back from true greatness, abundance, love, or financial prowess. As I'll tell you over and over throughout *Lust for Life*, I cannot make your goal for you; it's up to you. So if I speak about making money and that's not a goal right now, change it to making love, or making peace with yourself, and vice versa. Change the goals in this text and every text to always fit where you are in life, and as you read the book over and over, adjust. Never be rigid. The content I will speak on here will always allow you to reflect. I am never right. I am never the guru. I am an explorer with you, and I present these topics as such. I am never perfect; I am human. I make mistakes, plenty of them. The text here is being presented to you by a student of life, by a person who is not only hungry for life but also is ready to share real emotion, experience, thoughts, and stories. As a writer, I can only reach my goal if you promise me that you will engage with strangers, that you will believe in love, that you will seek to continue to explore how connected you are to nature. I am asking you to realize that you are not your job, you are not the designer jeans, and you are not that car that makes a hole in your wallet.

I used a very meticulous process to conglomerate the right words together, the words that you will need from time to time to find that inspiration. There are compounding thoughts set on experience, observation, education, emotions, intuition, introspection, and they all formulate a blended array of words that should propel us into the lanes of life that we truly deserve to live in— the lanes that we were born to live in, where there is harmony and internal peace, forever.

—Sylvester McNutt III

"We come into this world and think that we are coming into a world, instead of realizing that we are coming from it."

– Sylvester McNutt III, *Lust For Life*

"We live in a world where assumptions are more important than facts, and jumping to conclusions is more important than being patient and doing the research."

– Sylvester McNutt III, *Lust For Life*

"We are told to go to school for the first twenty to twenty-five years of our life just to come out in debt, trapped in a system where nobody understands finances, and are then expected to get a job that can support us and our families. I'm here to tell you that there are other alternatives; you don't have to follow the rules. Break them and find yourself."

– Sylvester McNutt III, *Lust For Life*

"To subjectively judge someone as you're getting to know him or her, without allowing the person complete space and reign to be his or her natural organic self, seems like an imposed prison for the person to live in. A prison of any kind seems to evoke hatred, conflict, depression, and sadness."

– Sylvester McNutt III, *Lust For Life*

"...reconnect to your earth, to your curiosities, to your complexities, to lust, to love, to passion, and to purpose."

– Sylvester McNutt III, *Lust For Life*

"I am never perfect; I am human. I make mistakes, plenty of them..."

– Sylvester McNutt III, *Lust For Life*

1: Choice

I sat on the edge of my bed in tears. She had just walked out of the door, it was raining, and the clouds were everywhere in the Arizona sky. I had so many thoughts that were going through my head. I was conflicted. I was confused. I was happy. I was curious. My ex-girlfriend of two years was asked to leave the apartment that she was invited to months earlier, by me; I had no choice because it was my only choice. I felt guilt. I didn't want her to be out in the world without my help or support. I bought her a plane ticket to fly back home, to Chicago, and offered her $1,000 cash so that she could figure things out.

She wanted neither; in fact, she only wanted me—even though she didn't act like it. It was hell living with her. Every moment, I was being yelled at and being told how I wasn't good enough; I felt like I was being attacked by someone who was supposed to protect me. I didn't want her to move in with me. We weren't ready. She lost her job, and none of her family members were in a position to help out. I knew for a fact that we were not ready to move in, but at the same time she was my girlfriend, and I didn't want her to be stranded or left for dead. I did what anyone with a heart would've done. I said, "Just move in here." She came for the holidays, and it was a great time, but after New Year's, everything went downhill. The graceful days turned into paltry nights of fighting and arguing. She wanted my attention at all times because she was codependent, she depended on me for her happiness. I had no idea what that was at the time, and if you don't know, a codependent relationship is one where one person relies on the other person for his or her identity, direction, happiness, and much more. As poets, we write things about how we want someone to be our everything, but in the real world, that can be problematic and can produce a codependent relationship. We should encourage our partners to have their own hobbies, friends, and activities to do outside of us. I was naïve and dumb about this at the time because I had never been with someone who was utterly obsessed with me and my every move. Of course, at first the narcissistic person inside each of us loves that someone thoroughly loves us inside and out. Go find me one person who will say he or she doesn't want another person to love him or her this holistically all the time, and I'll show you a damn liar. The love eventually turned into envy, because I had desires to make new friends and to expand myself with new activities. The love then turned into jealousy because of attention from other people. Her insecurities destroyed her inside and out, and these were insecurities that she had hidden well when I first met her. She was torn and broken, and she really couldn't stand men, which in retrospect makes me question why she even gave me the time of day. Her hatred for the male species surfaced, and she started treating me in a way that I didn't deserve. Everything I said started an argument; she was combative and very invasive —searching my personal cell phone, my work phone, my computer, and my notebooks where I kept my personal writings. She violated every ounce of privacy that I thought I deserved, all in the name of what she called love, and I thought this was awkward at best. I never went through her belongings because I am not insecure and had no desire to do that. I mean, if I claim that I love her, why would I search her stuff? That's what overbearing parents do to their adolescent children. That's what police do to drug dealers' houses after they get a warrant. How the hell is she claiming to love me while also reducing me to the kind of treatment that an adolescent or drug dealer would receive? I knew that I deserved better than this, and then I reached my breaking point. She woke me up yelling, screaming, and physically attacking me. She was trying to intimidate me and make me feel like a victim, but I am no fucking victim, no not me. I do not believe in violence in relationships. If I am going to physically hurt you, it is because you are my enemy and have put me in a position where I feel like my life is in danger. I will never allow anyone to corner me into a fight. I don't care who it is because I do not have the energy to fight anyone. I told her that she needed to pack her stuff and that she needed to leave. I was so serious about this, and of course, there was still love there on my end, so I bought her a ticket to go back home where I felt like she had more resources because her family was there. I tried to offer her money too so she could get back on her feet, and she told me that if I really loved her I wouldn't kick her out. Of course, I didn't listen to that manipulation tactic. You can't use the word "love" when you are treating someone like you hate him or her.

This section is the section on choice; don't forget that. We all have choices to make in our life. The choices that we make literally shape the experience of our life. If you do not take full accountability for your choices, you will always speak and act like a victim. Victims never love. Victims never feel. Victims are never happy. Victims are always broke. Victims are always victims because they think they deserve that, consciously or unconsciously. Some people will say that you should not place the blame or fault on the victim and that doing that is insensitive. That is not what I'm doing here. I'm placing power on anyone who is a victim; we all, at some point, will be a victim to something. When the situation occurs where we are placed into victimhood, we will stay there if we do not have the right skills, support, perspective, resources, or barriers set. In order to have abundance, and I mean to really have it, to really love life, and I mean to really have a lust for life, you have to be willing to make a choice. You have to be willing to make decisions over and over that will sow into your goal to attract and keep abundance. In the story I just shared, I had to make a decision, and some may say that it was a hard one, but to me it was not hard. She had to go. She had to go much quicker than she came. I made a decision that I deserved abundance; I made a decision that I deserved to be happy. I made a choice that a woman who wanted to fight me verbally, physically, and spiritually was not the type of woman that I deserved. I made a choice that I had to remove her from my life in order for me to see what else was possible. A lot of people stay because of the time invested, because of the years that have gone by, and because of the potential of how it could've been. Once you know what you deserve, and are ready to manifest it, you have to abolish everything and everyone who doesn't align with that.

Sitting on the edge of the bed crying, weeping, and pondering if I was making the right decision was a moment that I'll never forget. I thought about the public breakup that we were going to do on Facebook and the phone calls and text messages from so-called friends and family members. I thought about it all and when I came to a logical conclusion, I determined that I was allowing myself to feel things that were normal for this process. I decided that I need a woman who is going to lift me up and not tear me down. I made a choice that I was willing to let go of everything that was in my life because I didn't want to settle for just anything. This, to me, is step one to creating abundance, love, happiness, and richness. It all comes down to a choice. The power of choice, consciously or unconsciously, leads us down a life of destruction or happiness. It leads us to a life of power or victimhood. It leads us to abundance and happiness or down the abyss of nothingness. This is how powerful choice is. All we have is the power of choice.

What I notice is that the majority of people suffer because they don't understand the power of choice, and some believe that they do not actually have one. As a people, we are conditioned to give away our power, and that is why we suffer. To me, the ability to choose is the most important ability that a human must understand that he or she has. So to me, my only options are to create and sustain consistent happiness or to create and sustain consistent suffering via the choices I make. Either of those states belongs to my choices consciously or unconsciously. And that is the key to understand that our choices are conscious and unconscious; some philosophy arguments table in the thought of whether free will is truly free and whether it is being impressed upon us by an external force. Of course, we could debate about that until the end of time.

We make subconscious choices based on our conditioning, our beliefs, and our interpretation of the situations. But we have to be aware that we can interpret situations incorrectly, our beliefs can be grandiose and ridiculous, and our conditioning can be one based in fear or another extreme emotion that can cause us to misjudge. We also have the ability to change our beliefs, conditioning, and skills to interpret situations, but most of us do not, and those who do not, suffer. The only happy people I know, including myself, are people who have adapted to life as life has changed for them. This leads me to believe that rigidity does not hold as much value as agility. This makes me believe that no matter what value, belief, or moral we hold, sometimes we must revisit the purpose of it. We must do so if it is prohibiting us from happiness. So this leads me to the most important question that I ask myself daily: Do I have a choice? So do you believe that your destiny has been set? If you believe that your destiny has been set, then you also believe that you have no choice and that your life is nothing but an amalgamation of a design that has been given to you; do you believe that? I'm not saying that it is right or wrong to ask that; I'm simply introspecting and inquiring if that is the case. Do you believe that your plan has already been set? If so what is the purpose of your life? Is it just to fulfill some planned act you have no control over? If your life is already planned in order for the way it's supposed to be, then why do you have emotional outbursts when things go wrong or don't go the way in which you envisioned. I'm inquiring because I don't know; I am not above you in thought. I assume that you don't know either and that we are exploring this topic together. For me personally, I cannot believe that; I believe that I have a choice, that I have options, and that I have possibilities. I believe that I have a choice over my decisions in just about every single situation I enter. And I believe that regardless of my conditioning, my beliefs, or my consistent interpretation of situations, I have the ability to choose the *best* situation for me at that moment. Do you believe that too, and if possible, would it benefit you more to believe that?

The majority of people whom I come across in my line of work operate with what I called a victim mentality; with love and compassion, this is understandable because I do healing work. I do not say that to put them down or label them but to gain an understanding for the baseline of the logic that we need to rewire. They often feel like the world is against them; they feel like the world is a bad place; they feel like every bad thing that happens, only happens to them. Victims are accustomed to giving their power away. Victims wait for outside sources to guide or validate them. Victims do not know how to take control and lead themselves. The victim mind-set causes them to feel small, useless, and irrelevant. People who operate with a victim mind-set are often insecure in who they are because the world has shown them that whoever that is, he or she is not good enough. At some point in life, we are all victims of something, potentially major or minor. We have to be careful about labeling ourselves as victims once things happen to us; I see no value in doing that. It is important that when things happen that you observe them without grading and labeling them. It requires a higher level of consciousness to do this, but when you can simply observe everything, then you can become fully aware of the entire gravity of a situation. To assign meaning to everything that happens means that you will create a state of suffering because everything in your world has to have a definition or direction; it has to be black or white. The fact of the matter is this: in this world things occur naturally regardless of our understanding of them, and we so-called conscious beings have to accept these natural occurrences. Well, no, we don't have to, but we should, and when we don't, that is when we suffer. When we are unable to observe nature, changes, energy, facts, behaviors, and our thoughts, they control us—they take our choice. But when we observe to the deepest level, then we enable ourselves to tap into a new realm of choice. Tapping into a new realm of choice means accessing power over victimhood, richness over brokenness, and love over hate.

Step one in understanding choice is to understand that you always have a choice and that there are factors, conscious and unconscious, external and internal, that affect your choice. To say, "I didn't have a choice" is to commit perjury to yourself. There is always a choice, but the situation, your ability to reason, and the possible outcomes made you act in a certain way. I had a recent conversation that feels appropriate for this topic. I was in the barbershop getting my hair and beard lined up nicely for the weekend. Somehow, we got into the subject of the sport of boxing. As men, we love going to the barbershop so we can disagree with each other with often illogical arguments about sports and life. It's a moment of bonding and clarity for most of us. Somehow we got on the topic of a street fight, and the other guys in the barbershop mentioned that they would never run from a street fight, which is a comical situation to me. My logic is this: at no point in life do I want to experience pain, so in a street fight if I have to run, to me this is a valuable tactic. In most circles with men if you literally say that you would run from a fight, they will call you names or label you a coward or say that you are scared. I am perfectly OK with those labels; you can call me what you'd like. I told the man in the shop, "I don't have enough pride to fight anybody over anything." As long as you do not touch me, your words cannot provoke me. I will walk away from a fight nine times out of ten. The only reason I would actually fight is if you put your hands on me, which makes me feel like I have to defend myself. In my mind that situation doesn't happen often; the majority of it is men talking about what they will do or what they're going to do, and for me that is a sign that I can either talk my way out of it, or I can walk away. I told him how I cannot afford to get arrested, how I do not deserve to be in jail, how I do not deserve to feel pain, and how I do not desire to inflict pain upon other people. Yes, I have been in fights in my life, and it has taught me that it is not worth it. At this point in my life, I wish to avoid all physical fights with all human beings. With this as my logic, this is why I have no problem making the choice that I will walk away regardless of what those other men will call me. It does not impact my ego if they call me a coward or a pussy. I don't care enough about anyone's opinion of me because the person's opinion will never outweigh the opinion of a judge who decides that I should do a year behind bars for fighting. Do you get it now? See, some people feel like fighting is a justified response, especially if someone else *disrespects* you; I don't. And of course, in this example, we are using the act of physical fighting, but can you see how the same logic can apply to arguing and mental jostling with others? Oftentimes the perception that other people will take of you will trap you into making a choice that does not truly line up with who you are. This is why self-awareness is so important; it is more important to know who you are, to know yourself, and to trust yourself with the security of your identity than to be out walking in the world clueless. The majority of the people that you come across operate from a lower vibrational frequency than you; I am saying that simply because you are reading material like this. If that is true, it means that you have a duty to yourself to understand in the prep that there is always a choice. Be firm with this material; you may not have believed that there was always a choice because you were conditioned to possibly be a victim or something worse.

About a decade ago, while I was trying to leave college to find material that felt useful to my personal life, I stumbled across William Glasser's theory on choice. *In case you didn't pick up on that, the answer is no, I didn't find college to be as useful as I wanted it to be. However, while I was in college, I discovered a lot about my interests, what kind of person I was, and most importantly, I discovered that I could work on myself to make myself better. I learned more from the experience of college than the curriculum, and maybe that's what the big trick of it is. Maybe it's not about what we learn in books but what the books make us learn about ourselves.* He wrote a book in 1988 called *Choice Theory: A New Psychology of Personal Freedom,* and that book has ten principles on choice that I want to share here. They feel relevant for our dialogue on choice:

Ten Axioms of Choice Theory, by William Glasser

1. The only person whose behavior we can control is our own.
2. All we can give another person is information.
3. All long-lasting psychological problems are relationship problems.
4. The problem relationship is always part of our present life.
5. What happened in the past has everything to do with who we are today, but we can only satisfy our basic needs right now and plan to continue satisfying them in the future.
6. We can only satisfy our needs by satisfying the pictures in our quality world.
7. All we do is behave.
8. All behavior is total behavior and is made up of four components: acting, thinking, feeling, and physiology.
9. All behavior is choice, but we only have direct control over the acting and thinking components. We can only control our feelings and physiology indirectly through how we choose to act and think.
10. All total behavior is designated by verbs and named by the part that is the most recognizable.

"As poets, we write things about how we want someone to be our everything, but in the real world that can be problematic and can produce a codependent relationship. We should encourage our partners to have their own hobbies, friends, and activities to do outside of us."

—Sylvester McNutt III, *Lust for Life*

You can't use the word 'love' when you are treating someone like you hate them.

—Sylvester McNutt III, *Lust for Life*

"If you do not take full accountability for your choices, you will always speak and act like a victim. Victims never love. Victims never feel. Victims are never happy. Victims are always broke. Victims are always victims because they think they deserve that, consciously or unconsciously."

—Sylvester McNutt III, *Lust for Life*

"Once you know what you deserve, and are ready to manifest it, you have to abolish everything and everyone who doesn't align with that. You have to let go of the things that make you sad if you want to be happy. You have to learn from your failures if you want to be successful."

—Sylvester McNutt III, *Lust for Life*

"The only happy people I know, including myself, are people who have adapted to life as life has changed for them. This leads me to believe that rigidity does not hold as much value as agility. This makes me believe that no matter what value, belief, or moral we hold, sometimes we must revisit the purpose of it. We must do so if it is prohibiting us from happiness."

—Sylvester McNutt III, *Lust for Life*

"A lot of people stay because of the time invested, because of the years that have gone by, and because of the potential of how it could've been. Once you know what you deserve, and are ready to manifest it, you have to abolish everything and everyone who doesn't align with that."

—Sylvester McNutt III, *Lust for Life*

"It is important that when things happen that you observe them without grading and labeling them. It requires a higher level of consciousness to do this, but when you can simply observe everything, then you can become fully aware of the entire gravity of a situation."

—Sylvester McNutt III, *Lust for Life*

"The power of choice, consciously or unconsciously, leads us down a life of destruction or happiness. It leads us to a life of power or victimhood. It leads us to abundance and happiness or down the abyss of nothingness. This is how powerful choice is. All we have is the power of choice."

—Sylvester McNutt III, *Lust for Life*

"But when we observe to the deepest level, then we enable ourselves to tap into a new realm of choice. Tapping into a new realm of choice means accessing power over victimhood, richness over brokenness, and love over hate."

—Sylvester McNutt III, *Lust for Life*

"We have to destroy the victim mindset that may live inside of us. Victims are accustomed to giving their power away. Victims wait for outside sources to guide or validate them. Victims do not know how to take control and lead themselves. The victim mind-set causes them to feel small, useless, and irrelevant. People who operate with a victim mind-set are often insecure in who they are because the world has shown them that whoever that is, he or she is not good enough."

—Sylvester McNutt III, *Lust for Life*

"If something does not align with who you are, don't force it. You do not have to fight yourself in order to create peace; that is a state of war and conflict. You can walk away. You can let things go, and in fact, if it does not align at this moment, you should allow it to go."

—Sylvester McNutt III, *Lust for Life*

"You are allowed to break commitments if they are going to ruin you, your energy, or your life. Don't guilt yourself just because you need to change what you originally felt was a good idea."

—Sylvester McNutt III, *Lust for Life*

"You'll breathe so much better when you remove toxic people and mind-sets from your life. You deserve to feel lighter, happier, and full of life. Let go of the energy that no longer needs to be in your life."

—Sylvester McNutt III, *Lust for Life*

"Sometimes you have to choose other people, and sometimes you have to choose yourself. Just don't lose yourself in the process of choosing other people."

—Sylvester McNutt III, *Lust for Life*

If you have to say no, say no.
Don't make yourself feel bad
because of it, you don't own
the guilt, and you don't need
to feel down because of it.

—Sylvester McNutt III, *Lust for Life*

"Don't exhaust yourself because you feel like you have no choice or support, you always do. With consciousness and self-love, you'll always have yourself and the energy of the universe. Humans do not always know how to support others but if you believe in yourself, you'll show others how to believe in you."

—Sylvester McNutt III, *Lust for Life*

"When you're going through a tough time, always remember that there is one choice that nobody can take away. You always have the choice to bounce back, to recover, and to transcend your life to another realm."

—Sylvester McNutt III, *Lust for Life*

"If you're going through a tough time, always remember these two things: When there is a struggle in your life, that is the universe telling you that there is something that you have to let go of. And second, you have to be willing to take action to change your situation. Getting through adversity is only about your perspective and your action."

—Sylvester McNutt III, *Lust for Life*

"It feels good to let go of things that no longer want you, no longer need you, and no longer deserve your energy."

—Sylvester McNutt III, *Lust for Life*

"Step one in understanding choice is to understand that you always have a choice and that there are factors, conscious and unconscious, external and internal, that affect your choice. To say, "I didn't have a choice" is to commit perjury to yourself. There is always a choice, but the situation, your ability to reason, and the possible outcomes made you act in a certain way."

—Sylvester McNutt III, *Lust for Life*

"Love and happiness are not something that should be absent from your life. And if they are, that is OK, but I command you to get them back, and if you've never had them, you must believe that you have the skill to create them today. I command you to look at the people, the thoughts, the places, the routines that seem to be holding you back and attack them with vigor because you can change your life. Find out why you're allowing them to have weight in your life, and then, like a light switch, turn off what is no longer serving you. Once you disconnect from whatever is holding you back, go deep inside yourself, and discover who you truly are. A major part of this process will also require you to obtain new information; you will have to keep an open mind and an open heart."

—Sylvester McNutt III, *Lust for Life*

"Don't think that a tough times means it's time to break up with your lover. It's cliche, but it's so true: tough times don't last, tough people do. Don't quit, add new strategies to figure it out, have more conversations to go deeper into each other's minds. Make the choice to keep fighting together and never fight each other. You both will get through the tough time but you have to realize that you are on the same side."

—Sylvester McNutt III, *Lust for Life*

"No matter what friends and the internet say, if you want your relationships with other people to work, you will need a great deal of patience and forgiveness."

—Sylvester McNutt III, *Lust for Life*

Monday Affirmation on Choice

"The start of the week does not mean that we have to go back to a job or classroom that we hate. We must remember that we signed up for this position. In order for us to change it, we must dominate this current position. Monday is the day to set your intention, the day to tell yourself what the rest of the week will be about, and most importantly, it is the day to be grateful."

—Sylvester McNutt III, *Lust for Life*

Tuesday Affirmation on Choice

"Never allow a bad start to stop you from getting everything that you deserve. Everything is a process; the universe needs you to believe, and you have to trust the process in order to get everything that you truly deserve."

—Sylvester McNutt III, *Lust for Life*

Wednesday Affirmation on Choice

"People often fail at their goals because they fall short in the middle game. They lose steam; they lose motivation and purpose. Revisit your Monday. Revisit the reason why you are here to give yourself the boost that you need. You can get over the hump but you need genuine inspiration. You need to know your "why". Once you reconnect with your why it will be easy to know how to move."

—Sylvester McNutt III, *Lust for Life*

Thursday Affirmation on Choice

"Laziness runs rampant in this generation, and laziness's cousin is complacency. Don't get ready for the party yet because you haven't put in enough work. You haven't exhausted yourself enough. You haven't bled enough. You haven't cried enough. You haven't broken enough bones on the way to everything that you claim you want."

—Sylvester McNutt III, *Lust for Life*

Friday Affirmation on Choice"

"You have the choice to party, and you have the choice to keep building. You have the choice to join your friends who want to blow money, waste time, and opportunity, or you can use it to get better. You can use this moment to get back in the gym, to get to the office, or to work on your brand. You can use this moment to strengthen your love with your lover with an intense conversation and night of romance. Do not waste Fridays on the party, because it's not time for that."

—Sylvester McNutt III, *Lust for Life*

Saturday Affirmation on Choice

"Use this day to dedicate it to friends, to family, to service, to make the lives of people better. Consider Saturdays to be your completely selfless days. Start with your lover. Go find them and serve them. If you're single, go be of service to your best friends, whatever that looks like. Take care of everyone in your life, and then take care of yourself last."

—Sylvester McNutt III, *Lust for Life*

Sunday Affirmation on Choice

"Sunday Funday means look back on your hard work this week, and appreciate it. It means to toast to the times that you'll forget with the people whom you'll never forget. It means to drink more mimosas, eat more brunch, watch more football, travel, and live your life before it passes you by. Sunday means to give thanks, to be grateful, and to reenergize yourself with the presence of beautiful people."

—Sylvester McNutt III, *Lust for Life*

2: How to Free Your Mind

In order to free your mind, you have to accept that you have a choice in just about every situation to decide what you're going to do and how you're going to react to the situation. You must ask yourself, is it possible that I can override my conditioning, therefore taking complete control of my life? Is this possible? The hardest part about choice is sometimes we feel like we do not have a choice, and the reason we do not have a choice is because of our conditioning. We have automatic responses to situations, to phrases, and to sayings that people spew at us. These words are conjugated in a way that tangles our emotions. Someone may say that overriding your conditioning is hard, and that assessment is correct, but telling yourself that something is hard actually makes it harder, and gives it the life it needs to feel true. You never have to tell yourself that something is difficult; instead you must ask like I have been doing here, is it possible? Don't label anything as hard because it is trapping your mind instead of freeing your mind. So is it possible to free your mind? Say your answer aloud. What happens if you tell yourself that you're capable of doing something? Doesn't it seem plausible that you could actually achieve it?

This is why you must start with the question, *"Is it possible?"*

In order to free your mind, you have to block out the things that society has given you about who you cannot be, what you cannot do, and the reasons why you are unworthy. You must always tell yourself that you are worthy. You must always ask yourself, is this possible? You must always question everything, all the time, everywhere you go—this is how you free your mind. Your body will always remain trapped as long as your mind operates in a limiting way. Your body is the physical manifestation of your mind, and your mind is the mental manifestation of your body. They balance each other; they work hand in hand, and they need each other to operate at their highest frequencies. Your body craves nutrition, hydration, flexibility, and breathing. Your mind craves learning, thought, and introspection. Do not allow yourself to enslave one or the other; they both need to be totally free in order for you to feel consistent abundance. I'm asking you to abolish what other people—church, religion, parents, teachers, schools, gurus, and media figures—have given you. Do not simply believe what people say because they have a title that supposedly places them above you; that's just stupid and irresponsible of you as a truth seeker. I feel overwhelmingly compelled to share and to introspect a situation that I experienced with my parents as a youth. I feel this is a common situation that many people go through and hope that through this story you can relate to your own journey, taking the pieces of my story that you need and discarding what does not serve you.

My mother and father believed that to make it in this world, you have to go to college and obtain a degree. Their perception was that the degree would then lead to a good job, which would result in good pay, and that would enable me take care of myself and my family if I eventually created one. There is nothing wrong with this mind-set, but to me it's outdated, and it truly does not align with who I am and who I want to be. I knew that school felt like a big waste of time to me; literally, every second of it felt like hell. When I was young, I would write poems and stories in my notebooks while the teachers were talking. They would call on me because they thought I wasn't paying attention, but somehow I was, and I would insert the answers to their questions calmly. I never raised my hand in class. I didn't care. I was indifferent in school. I like talking to girls, so the social aspect was pretty awesome because there are so many girls in school, but learning? No, I don't feel as if the pace was ever fast enough for me or the style. In school they make you take written tests to prove your mastery level of the presented material.

To me, this is flawed because they do not incorporate everyone's learning style or ways of expression. For example, if you could give me the material and I could simply explain it to you with words, there is nothing that I wouldn't pass. But when you give me a Scantron sheet and give me four answers that are very similar, sometimes my brain gets lost in the translation. Math. I hate math. I remember being in a class where the math also included letters. They called it algebra or something disrespectful like that. I knew that I was never going to be a great student because I became indifferent to school at a very young age. My parents kept drilling in my head that I needed to go to college. They drilled in my head that college was the most important thing because it gave you an upper hand over the competitors, who are people who are also trying to make money and take care of their families. Again, this logic for them worked, and I cannot fault them for passing it down to me. I'm not teaching my kids that. I don't believe in college alone as your source of experience; for me, even though I did my 120 hours for the degree. It's important to combine education, experience, and most importantly new perspectives as you grow. I hope you realize and accept that I am not a fan of college, schools, or the US education system. This is not a persuasive argument here. I truly don't care if you do go to college or not. I am not shaming college, in fact, I needed college to get to where I am. I care about you figuring out what skills you have, and I care that you use them. I care that you figure out what your passions are and that you chase them, no matter what that journey looks like. For some, college can offer you a great deal of skill and perspective to help you find your passions. I am not ignorant to the fact that some people benefit greatly from college. In my situation, I knew at a young age that I had a special set of skills and charisma, to write and to talk to people. I knew when I was about fourteen years old that I wanted to be a public speaker and an author. I played football, so of course, I had that dream as well because what athlete doesn't want to play at the professional level? I knew that having a job that didn't align with my skills and my passions would cause me to feel enslaved, and I knew that wasting my talents would cause me to live in a constant place of sadness and regret. There is nothing wrong with having a job. There is a lot wrong with having a unique skill, talent, or passion, and wasting it. I had to free my mind, and don't forget that this is our subject here.

My parents had a strategy and ideas for how I should live my life, and so they engrained a bunch of different thoughts and ideas in me about who and how I should be. Parents are supposed to do that, I suppose. They never gave me support or motivation to be an entrepreneur, and they hated that I hated school. They hated how outspoken I was about how much I hated going to school. I told them in high school that I wanted to start a lawn-care business and drop out of high school. Again, I'm not good at math, but I told them if I charge twenty dollars per lawn and did one hundred lawns a week, I would be making $2,000 a month. They told me that that was too much work and that the business would fail. Mind you, my grandfather successfully ran a lawn-care business that I and my dad worked at every summer when I was a younger kid, so that was my inspiration. I watched every move my grandfather made. I watched him jot down notes about whose lawn was next, who owed, and the strategy that we needed as a crew to be efficient. I didn't know it then, but as I type, in retrospect, it all made sense. I loved cutting grass, doing hedges, and pulling up weeds. It wasn't really the job, but for me it was the deep satisfaction that came with doing the job, with seeing how happy we made people, and how much ownership we took over every lawn as an artist and as a business. I did the job with my grandfather when I was younger than twelve. So when I was fourteen and I told my parents that I wanted my own lawn-care business, they told me that I needed to stay in school and go to college. Again, they were conditioning me to believe that school was the most valuable thing, and again, they're not wrong. However, it doesn't and didn't align with me, and this is why I am telling you to reject what people tell you. You have to; otherwise you wouldn't be reading this book. I'd be stuck at a job that I hated, with debt, with a woman who didn't really love me, and I would be looking for a way to find abundance and bliss. You would be reading someone else's books, and we might even pass each other on the street as strangers. Don't let your life go by living in the shadows of other people's thoughts on how your life should go. It's your life, and you get to choose how it's going to go. You have the inalienable right to decide how you want your experience to go. If you want abundance, peace, and love, then you must decide that this is what you are worthy of. If there is something that you desire and it is outside of the spectrum of what others want for you, be ready for pushback, be ready for problems, and be ready to go your own path alone. Most likely, they're not going to support this mission. That doesn't make them bad people for your life; it just means they're not good for your dreams. To free your mind, you have to understand that other people truly believe that they know how to live life, and most people believe that they know how to do it better than you. Even though I, the writer, am telling you not to listen to them, that doesn't mean I know what I am talking about either. I am begging you to reject everyone's thoughts and perspectives as you dig deep to discover what you want, who you want to be, and what kind of life you want to live. Reject the authors, reject the gurus, reject the parents, reject the governments, and most importantly reject the media's ideal on how you are supposed to be. Use your brain. I'm not telling you that other people do not have great advice and wisdom and valuable information, because we know that many people do. We are talking about you resetting your brain, taking your life to the next level, and resetting the thoughts that you have believed in. The challenge is to take a spiritual inventory of what you believe in. Figure out what makes sense and what doesn't, and what no longer makes sense, you discard because it doesn't serve your purpose. If there is something that you want, like love, riches, or happiness that doesn't fade, there is something that you have to be willing to give up. I'll bet my next meal that one of the things you need to give up is a particular mind-set or belief that is holding you back. Are you ready to give up things that you may have believed in for a decade or more? Until the answer is yes, you're not ready to live fully in your light, in your purpose, or in a lane of consistent abundance.

Challenge

In conclusion, with my story, going against what my parents taught me worked for me, but I didn't reject every single thought they gave me. Again, I knew my purpose at a young age. I knew exactly what I wanted to do, so everything that didn't align was kicked to the wayside. Many people struggle to figure out what they want in the long term because they simply don't know what they want in the moment, and the long term game has everything to do with the current moment. It's as simple as knowing what you want in the moment. You're allowed to change what you want out of life as life changes. You don't need a ten- or twelve-year plan; you simply need a consistent plan for the moment, a plan that allows you flexibility to grow from each moment to the next. The reason that I can offer you thoughts on love, abundance, and freeing your mind is because I took the journey myself. And when I came out on this other end, I felt an overwhelming energy over my soul that commanded me to express these thoughts here. The energy told me that if I do not create words that cut deep but uplift, words that inspire while conjuring thought, words that punish you for your laziness but motivate you for your effort, then I would be wasting my talent. I'm writing *Lust for Life* because I genuinely enjoy every single day that I have on this earth. I have no stress. I have no complaints. Well, I could go on about the government, racism, and people who put the tissue on the roll in the wrong direction, but that's not my angle as a writer or human being. I'll leave that to other people to debate and figure out what is right or wrong. My angle is to ask you simple questions like this: Do you deserve to feel abundance when you wake up, do you deserve to feel peace when you go to sleep, and do you deserve to have a lust for life? Here's my challenge for you, and I want you to annoy everyone on your social-media time line today, tomorrow, and whenever else you feel like it. I want you to post a picture of yourself reading this book.

I will not lie to you here, so please accept both reasons why this matters. I want to talk about you first and me second. I want you to post this book. I want you to use the hashtags on your preferred social networks, #LustforLife and #SylvesterMcNutt. In the caption I want you to write about your journey, about love, about happiness, and abundance, and peace, and joy— not for me but because I want you to manifest these things through the world. We all use social media, and if we make a 1 percent shift in how we use social media, it can make a 100 percent difference in our lives; this I know for a fact because if it weren't for social media, you wouldn't have even bought this book. If you're one of those who go straight to the point and you don't like leaving long captions on social media, don't change. Just use this phrase, "Lust for Life." Please do this; share the picture, so your friends and family can support or be jealous—that is their choice— this post is apart of your journey to acquire everything that you deserve. I will do my best to like, to comment, and to share every image that I can because I am going to do my best to support you too. I told you that I had a personal reason for this too. I am an entrepreneur, and I live solely off my words. I cannot predict the future, and I have no idea if I'll be able to sustain myself and my kids off my words forever—that is my goal, but we all know life gives us scenes that we cannot predict. I am humbly asking, as an independent author, as a human, and as an entrepreneur, that you not only post about *Lust for Life* but you also tell people about it. Doing this will help me stay alive, stay relevant as a writer, and will ensure that new people check out my words that may save their life. Friends, I've heard in the past that some people binge on my books and try to read them in one sitting. I can't say that strategy is wrong or ineffective; hell, I'm sure with all of your busy lives, you have to do what you have to do, but I challenge you to really write down and share your thoughts on what we have talked about so far. If you don't have a safe place to share them, just e-mail them to me.

What does it mean to you to free your mind, and what are some things that you need to let go of? What does it mean to you to make choices, and do you have complete control over your choices? This is a compounding piece of literature here where each concept builds off on the next. Find a safe space to share your findings like a journal, a YouTube video, an e-mail thread to friends, or again simply send it to me, and if my schedule allows me to, I will respond to as many as I can.

"To free your mind, you must question everything that has ever been said to you, even if you said it to yourself. You must reject everything about your belief system, no matter how hard that task sounds."

—Sylvester McNutt III, *Lust for Life*

"To free your mind, you must always ask yourself, is it possible? As long as you can answer, yes, it is possible, then and only then will you be able to take the next steps toward freedom by learning something new or experiencing something that you've never seen before."

—Sylvester McNutt III, *Lust for Life*

"Don't let your life go by living in the shadows of other people's thoughts on how your life should go. These people are confused, scared, and are not willing to put themselves out there. You have to live. You have to risk it all. You have to go hard. You have to free your mind. You have to earn everything that you desire. Not only can you do it but you will do it the second that you stop listening to outsiders because the only relevant thoughts occur inside you."

—Sylvester McNutt III, *Lust for Life*

"I'll bet my next meal that one of the things you need to give up is a particular mind-set or belief that is holding you back. Are you ready to give up things that you may have believed in for a decade or more? Until the answer is yes, you're not ready to live fully in your light, in your purpose, or in a lane of consistent abundance."

—Sylvester McNutt III, *Lust for Life*

"The challenge is to take a spiritual inventory of what you believe in and how you view the world. Figure out what makes sense and what doesn't, and what no longer makes sense, you discard because it doesn't serve your purpose anymore. It's perfectly OK to withdraw a commitment if it no longer aligns with you. It's OK to believe in something with the information you have but to discard it as you grow and as you become who you are meant to be. Never feel like you have to be a certain way because of what you once were."

—Sylvester McNutt III, *Lust for Life*

"If there is something that you desire and it is outside of the spectrum of what others want for you, be ready for pushback, be ready for problems, and be ready to go your own path alone. Most likely, they're not going to support you on this mission. That doesn't make them bad people for your life; it just means they're not good for your dreams. And since they're not good for your dreams, you have to distance yourself from them."

—Sylvester McNutt III, *Lust for Life*

"Many people struggle to figure out what they want in the long term because they simply don't know what they want in the moment, and it's as simple as knowing what you want in the moment. Never obsess about the future and long-terms goals, especially if you don't know. You're allowed to focus on the moment. You're allowed to change what you want out of life as life changes. You don't need a ten- or twelve-year plan; you simply need a consistent plan for the moment, a plan that allows you flexibility to grow from each moment to the next."

—Sylvester McNutt III, *Lust for Life*

"Free your mind. Stop thinking that living check to check is normal. Stop thinking that being broke is just the way it is. You deserve abundance, but it's up to you to create it. Step one to getting out of debt is to believe that you no longer deserve to suffer. You'll have to create a budget, you'll have to live within your means, and you'll have to accept that it's more important to keep your money than to spend it on useless things. Free your mind, focus on staying debt-free, and increase your income."

—Sylvester McNutt III, *Lust for Life*

"In order to free your mind, you have to block out the things that society has given you about who you cannot be, what you cannot do, and the reasons why you are unworthy."

—Sylvester McNutt III, *Free Your Mind*

"This society is set up to trap you in a box, a box that limits and marginalizes your talents and belief in self. It doesn't want you to believe in yourself because powerful people break the mold—they want you to be a mindless person who never questions anything. However, this is the best time in the history of humankind to believe in yourself. There is a unique creative space and a multitude of abundant opportunities here, where you can literally be what or who you want to be, if you're willing to put in the work. Your mission is to abolish society's perspectives, and figure out who and what you are. This journey may take time; don't let them box you into some limiting, defeating label. *Be free.*"

—Sylvester McNutt III, *Free Your Mind*

"You cannot achieve the life that you desire until you let go of self-hate, disbelief, and pessimistic mind-sets. Let it go, so you can grow."

—Sylvester McNutt III, *Free Your Mind*

"If anger is always present in your life, it will always control you, and anger is not an emotion that creates healthy outcomes. Learn to free yourself from anger before it enslaves you. Let it go; it's not worth it."

—Sylvester McNutt III, *Free Your Mind*

"I knew that having a job that didn't align with my skills and my passions would cause me to feel enslaved, and I knew that wasting my talents and time would cause me to live in a constant place of sadness and regret. I believe that you have a duty to yourself to have that awareness, to understand who you are, and to always go after what you want. I believe that you should free your mind and at least try chasing your dreams."

– Find The Right Career, Sylvester McNutt III

"I'm asking you to abolish what other people—church, religion, parents, teachers, schools, gurus, and media figures—have given you. Do not simply believe what people say because they have a title that supposedly places them above you; that's just stupid and irresponsible of you as a truth seeker. I am asking you to discover your own truth, to live in that truth, and never step outside of your truth. But this is a challenge because most of us do not live there, so can you do it? Can you find yourself? Can you become who you're supposed to become or will you remain bogged down by everyone else's truth, even if it feels like a lie?"

– Sylvester McNutt III, *Free Your Mind*

"Happiness is a state inside you that wants and needs you to live there. There will be people and outside sources that try to rob you of this. Don't get mad at them because that is energy that you do not deserve. You deserve to let it go, so your mind and body can move in peace."

—Sylvester McNutt III, *Free Your Mind*

"An overwhelming majority of the people that you will interact with are unreasonable and unruly; this is why elevating your consciousness is so important. It's paramount that you are the wise one, the one who observes everything, who gathers facts, and who acts only after that process has occurred."

—Sylvester McNutt III, *Free Your Mind*

And when external forces try to destroy you, you must repeat this phrase to heal yourself, "They do not have the ability to defeat me. This moment of adversity will subside, and no matter what, I will overcome."

—Sylvester McNutt III, *Free Your Mind*

"When anger, jealousy, guilt, and other powerful emotions set in, ask yourself if the energy is necessary for you to hold. If it is not, you must let that negative energy go quicker than it came."

—Sylvester McNutt III, *Free Your Mind*

"Trust. What a simple word that contains the most complex, the deepest, and the strongest feelings that we have. One thing that you must always do is trust yourself, even after mistakes, because a mistake doesn't mean that you're unworthy of abundance. A mistake is your path to learn and to grow, your path to be a better human than you were yesterday. Trust that you will learn, that you will grow, and that you will get better through the experience. You don't need any self-doubt to seep in because it will destroy you; forgive yourself, so you can trust yourself again; you deserve that."

—Sylvester McNutt III, *Free Your Mind*

"If you look out into the future for guidance, it will trap your mind. The possibilities of what things can be will dominate your present moment, and you won't be able to live in the now. If you look behind to the past, the mistakes will eat you alive because you'll think that you should've known better. Be kind and forgiving to your journey. Mistakes happen, and we don't know if the future we see is even going to happen. Be grateful for this moment. Keep your mind here, not in the past or in the future, and do the very best that you can with this moment."

—Sylvester McNutt III, *Free Your Mind*

In order to keep your mind free, you must meditate, and if meditation scares you, that is OK because you're allowed to have fear. Simplify the process. You can be anywhere on the planet doing anything, and you can stop for six-seconds to breathe and release.

This is meditation.

Meditation is the art of stopping what you are doing so you can stay present, so you can take deep breaths of new oxygen, and so you can simply let go of the weight of the world. Just breathe, for six-seconds.

—Sylvester McNutt III, *Free Your Mind*

"One of the keys to freeing your mind is to declutter the people who you're allowing to give you energy. There is always a possibility that you must unfriend, unfollow, and dissociate from those who are harmful. You are allowed to become uncommitted and go away if you have to save yourself. Please save yourself."

—Sylvester McNutt III, *Free Your Mind*

"From the outside looking in, you may call me selfish, and you're right; I am selfish. I've come to be this way because I am a giver, and I will never stop giving, loving, and serving other people. If I have a loaf of bread, then you are going to get half; if I am the only friend with a car, then everyone has a ride, and if I am the only one with a house, then everyone has a place to sleep. I've put money in people's hands and never asked for a dollar in return. Giving doesn't hurt me at all; it's what I am here to do. So at times, I will be selfish; I will put me first, and I will not explain why I am taking a "me" moment. At the core of who I am, I am a giver, so if anyone has an issue with me taking a me moment, then they need to be removed from my space until they understand me better."

—Sylvester McNutt III, *Free Your Mind*

"There is time. There is experience. There is practice. There is fear. There is jealousy. There is hate. There are many descriptions and stories that we tell ourselves. Some wrong, some right, some impactful, and some not. At the end of it all, do not allow any of it to deviate you away from a happy life. There is nothing more important than doing everything you can to create and sustain a happy life."

—Sylvester McNutt III, *Free Your Mind*

"Social media and text messaging have the power to instantly change your mood. This can be good or bad; it just depends on who and what is allowed to enter your phone. Be mindful of who you follow, what you watch, and who can reach you through the device, and if you have to cut off the energy from reaching you, do it."

—Sylvester McNutt III, *Free Your Mind*

"We give out our phone numbers freely, and it's time to stop. Everyone doesn't need your number or access to you. Your energy is more important than having people in your life who only text you when they're bored or if they need something from you."

—Sylvester McNutt III, *Free Your Mind*

"You don't need more followers or more friends; you need more recharging, more reading, more introspection, more time to yourself to dive deep into your inner world, more time to reconnect with the energy that molds you, the energy that helps you have a great life."

—Sylvester McNutt III, *Free Your Mind*

"When your mind becomes clogged with Garbage, hit the reset button, and throw it all away. Wipe your phone. Stay off-line. Change your number, and get back to your workout routine. You need a clean life, a clean diet, and a clean mind. You're allowed to dump what is no longer serving your life. If you have to throw it all away to create a better you, then do it, and do it now. Don't wait for a miracle to save you. Save yourself."

—Sylvester McNutt III, *Free Your Mind*

"You will get peace of mind once you create distance between yourself and anyone who has proven to be a wolf."

—Sylvester McNutt III, *Free Your Mind*

"Here's a life lesson on paper that I hope you learn before it is too late. You can be open, honest, and transparent with who you are, but you can still reserve and hold back information from people who do not deserve it. Yes, we claim that we crave honesty, but some people don't know how to handle it. Some don't care to handle valuable information, and these people will use any information they can to hurt you, to damage your life, and your reputation. Be smart, and use your discernment when you let people in close to you. Nothing is more important than peace of mind and happiness."

—Sylvester McNutt III, *Free Your Mind*

Stop believing in things that don't believe in you. Stop going back to situations that feel like hell when you deserve heaven.

—Sylvester McNutt III, *Free Your Mind*

"I learned a long time ago that I don't have enough patience to deal with savages and coldhearted people. I care too much about too many things. Now, I just let the fucking savages destroy each other, and I'm mindful of where and who I spend my days with."

—Sylvester McNutt III, *Free Your Mind*

"Some people believe that you should be honest all the time, with everyone you come across, about everything. And if you believe that, you are either a child or you haven't lived much life. Deception is and will always be a major part of business, of relationships, and of life. The food companies lie to us about ingredients. The government lies to us about money and war. Our parents lie to us about made-up fairy tales and fables because they want us to be happy. In dating, people lie from the first date about who they really are because they want to win us. If you freely omit all of yourself, and freely give the world access to you, you are simply opening yourself up to their lies. I'm not telling you to lie; I am telling you to be mindful of who and what you're dealing with at all times. Peace of mind is more important than trying to change a corrupt, mad world. Let them be; you stay over here, and breathe."

—Sylvester McNutt III, *Free Your Mind*

"Believe in love. I'm not talking about fairy tales and movies. I am talking about the love that has always been and will always be inside you. Believe in that."

—Sylvester McNutt III, Lust For Life

3: Why and How You Must Find Your Purpose

Everyday someone asks me, "Sylvester, what drives you?" And I never have an answer for this question. I want to use this section to explain the inner workings of my mind, so you can understand how I found my purpose, how I found my happiness, and how I became the person that I am from a "purpose" perspective.

I can't tell you why I stay up until six or seven in the morning writing. I can't tell you why I read forty to fifty books per year. I can't tell you why I write multiple books at once, while making money off books from years ago, when most people would just sit back and be content with that money, while touring and spreading inspiration. If I could only use one word, I would say, "purpose," but for a person who is truly trying to find himself or herself, we both know that won't suffice.

I feel like I have superhero-like inspiration. Spider-Man goes out every day to fight bad guys because of the regret he feels for not stopping that bad guy when he had the chance. The bad guy eventually killed his uncle, and that drove him to seek revenge, with a preventive and protective twist. Batman, a millionaire by day, goes out every single night, so he can keep the criminals off the streets. He is driven by the fact that his parents were murdered because of a criminal mastermind. For me, maybe watching my parents destroy each other through divorce is my angle. Maybe dealing with racism, the bouts of heartbreak, or the feeling like I never had enough to make others happy drives me. I don't really have an answer that I can explain to you. I do know that I have purpose, and my sense of purpose drives me to keep going no matter how successful I think I am. I know that there is so much more that I can do, so many more places to travel to, and I have so much more to learn. I'm at a point in my speaking career where I'm selling out the meeting spaces that used to be hard to fill, but it's simply not enough for me yet. I'm ready to go to bigger venues, and honestly, I am not afraid of the journey. I want to be able to do speaking engagements in Madison Square Garden, inside the United Center, and inside the Staples Center. I know that it is going to take me decades to manifest this version of my dream. I am willing to work for it, I am willing to humble myself for it, and I am willing to fail over and over, until I get it perfect, and I accept that it will never be perfect. It will never be perfect, but since my craft is writing and speaking, I am willing to make as many errors as it takes, so I can create the most perfect product possible.

I don't have days where I am more inspired than others. I am always inspired to do what I am doing, and that is because I am living fully inside my *purpose*. When you are inside your purpose and you have a good system, it never feels like work. You might be suffering with your purpose because you feel like your job is not fulfilling, and that is where I have to stop you. Whoever said that your job is supposed to be your purpose? I'm fortunate that people pay me for what I do, but I started writing just to clear my mind, to sort through all of my thoughts, and to help me understand the way this world works. I started sharing my writings because I said to myself, "Maybe someone else can benefit from my crazy-ass thoughts." I didn't start doing this for money. This statement sounds fictional, but I had no idea that I was good enough to earn a living by following my dream when I was not following it. But I knew that the only way I would be happy was if I woke up every day and followed my passion, which is to write, to speak about the human condition, and to explore people's lives with words. Money came later once I stepped all the way into my purpose. Once I quit my corporate job and decided that I wanted to serve the world through my writings full time, that is when my happiness went to an unreal level. I quit because I wasn't enjoying my job, and I wanted more time to write books, because a part of me felt like I needed to be all the way in for it to work. It wasn't about money because I didn't understand how money actually worked back then, nor did I have any money when I started. It was really about passion and how I felt when other people read my stuff, and I just wanted more people to read my thoughts, my perspectives, and my poetry. If the money stops coming in, yes, I know I would have to get some type of job or create a new business, but it would have to be connected to what I'm doing now because I know what makes me happy. Talking with people about life and challenging their thoughts gives me the most fulfillment. So if you're suffering to find yourself, or your purpose, or the right job fit, maybe you're looking at it all wrong. Maybe you're too worried about the money. Maybe your solution is to keep your job and use your off time more wisely. Maybe you should start a business on the side and do that when you're not at work. Or maybe you need to go rogue and just quit, figure yourself out, and risk it all doing what you love whether thats a new job or entrepreneurship.

Questions To Help Find Your Purpose

What really drives you? What really gives you a sense of fulfillment, or happiness, of belonging? That's where you need to go. If you really enjoy tech and you're working in customer service as an insurance salesperson, my question is, why? Don't tell me that you have to pay bills and that you have all this stuff that you need to pay for. All of that is a choice. You can make your life much cheaper, but you haven't committed to that choice and because of your unwillingness to minimize your lifestyle, you feel stuck at a job that doesn't serve you. Don't make excuses; just make changes, and keep growing as a human being. If your purpose is to paint, to sing, to draw, to smile, to make tacos, or to read one hundred books per year, you have to make a choice that nothing will stop you from making your dreams a reality. This starts with a choice. Do you want it? Yes or no?

You know what really drives me? A sense of accomplishment, but at the same time, it doesn't. An accomplishment is really a destination, and I'm not a fan of obsessing about titles and destinations. Those things limit people. I am a fan of the journey. I am a fan of the process. I am a fan of taking nothing and turning it into something. I get a sense of accomplishment from moving forward in a journey and moving up through each process. This helps give me a daily purpose. Some people get lost in the idea that the having or finding your purpose means it will rule you forever. I don't feel as if that is realistic or true. It's important that we remember that life goes through phases, and each phase brings us different challenges and different levels of happiness. This is why it's so important that we find a daily purpose, and we reach our goals after we grow and move on in life. When I was in college, my purpose felt like it was to grow out of being an introvert and to figure out how to be more social. I was an extreme introvert in college who dealt with extreme anger and had a mean streak. I was not a nice human being at all, unless it was a girl talking to me; then I would flirt and be myself. But if a girl was not interested in me, then I didn't care about having a conversation with anyone. Today, that human being I described is different. He is completely opposite: nonviolent, an extrovert, who is consistently reminding himself to be himself. I don't have kids yet, and I want kids, at least two, but no more than two (watch the universe reward us with triplets just because I said no more than two). When and if I do have kids, I can guarantee you that my purpose will change. My purpose will shift toward being a great father, a great leader, and supporting my woman through the journey of parenthood. A lot of people think that finding your purpose means finding the one thing that you can or will do forever, and I just illustrated to you why I don't believe that ideology is logical. I also detailed to you three different points of my life where my purpose has been vastly different; am I any different from you? Of course not, so why do you think that you only have one singular purpose on this planet? Moving forward, if you feel like this will impact you in a more efficient way, please stop thinking that you have one singular purpose. Please stop thinking that your purpose has to pay you, because it's that type of rhetoric that has ruined people's lives and perceptions of who they are.

I want to make my stance perfectly clear. I believe that we have skills, and we have passions. Sometimes we are lucky enough to have a job that allows us to combine both. Sometimes we have to do something we are good at, even if we don't enjoy every aspect of it. My advice is to appreciate the skill set and the opportunity that you have. Your job may not be your "purpose," and it doesn't have to be; your job can simply be something that you're good at doing that helps you take care of yourself, your family, and your desires in life.

Finding Success Inside Your Passion

I believe that to be really successful in life you must enjoy the process of it all, and when you no longer enjoy the process, you have to move on. In my profession, writing a book is a long and very draining process if you're not methodical in your ways. Every writer has a process, and I've never shared mine, but I'll do that here. Maybe this will actually help if anyone is an aspiring entrepreneur or writer, or if you just want to take what I've done and apply to your own journey.

I won't lie here. I'm not one of those people who wakes up at four or five in the morning. I know a lot of entrepreneurs preach about how they get up early and how you shouldn't sleep in. I agree, and there have been times in my life when I would get up at five o'clock to write for three to four hours. Today I don't do that, and the reason why I want to share my current process is because it is the healthiest. Gurus and entrepreneurs like me always preach that you should beat your craft over the head, and I agree, but it has to be done in a healthy and efficient way, it has to be done in a way that works for you. My natural body clock wants me to go to bed around four or five in the morning and it wants me to get up around noon or one p.m. I ignore my natural body clock because I found another alternative that works for me. One thing that I learned from working as a manager in corporate America is that if you do not have an efficient system to run yourself and your organization, you will suffer, and your productivity will never rise.

These days I get up between seven thirty and nine o'clock. I never use an alarm clock. I allow my body to get a full night of sleep every night. The reason I get up around these hours is because the person that I spend the most time with has these hours so I adopted her schedule so I could be flexible, but at my core, I'd rather stay up late and get up late. I believe that's the first step in being healthy, to allow your natural body clock to wake up. When I wake up, depending on what my bladder says, I'll go to the kitchen or the bathroom. The first thing I do is drink at least twelve ounces of water. Then I'll stretch for ten to fifteen minutes. I do this flow every morning because it gets my body flowing and my brain going. It's simple, and since I travel a lot, I can do this anywhere in the world. Seventy-five percent of the time I'll make my bed, which I should do every single morning, but I'm consistent for the most part. The reason why I make my bed is because I cannot tolerate living in a dirty house. The temple and your vehicle should always be clean. There's so much energy that goes on at your house, and keeping it clean is one of the keys to happiness, to reducing anxiety, to manifesting a positive vibe, and to increasing productivity. I don't care what job you have or what you're trying to create, but you need a morning routine.

Some days I go to the gym in the morning because I like to start the day with the sweat and weights, especially later in the morning because the traffic is light, and that gives me as much time as I need to get in and out of the gym without conflict. Some days I wait until the afternoon to go because I play basketball for the cardiovascular component.

After I get my gym work in, the first thing I do is create a plan for the day. No matter how much I have to do, I always create a plan even if my plan is just to relax and recharge. I like to call it "setting my intention." While I create a plan, I focus on simplicity. I do not like to-do lists that have seventeen different items on them. That's a bit excessive to me, and I personally never feel like I can accomplish anything if there are fifteen things that I have to do today. I keep it simple and short. I never make a to-do list that has more than five activities on it for the day. I know my long-term goals, and I know how much activity is needed to create them. However, the long-term game requires so much action and so many baby steps that I never focus on it. I never ever focus on long-term goals. It seems stressful, unproductive, and like a waste of mental energy. For example, I recently established a Roth IRA investment account for retirement.

Essentially, having that account is a long-term financial plan right? Most of us would agree that there are long-term financial goals that we should have, and I agree that we should, but I refuse to obsess about it. I believe this is why I am much happier than a lot of the people whom I speak to. They obsess about long-term goals, and I see no value in that. Yes, they do matter; if they matter to you, I would never try to tell you that your long-term goals don't matter. But my logic tells me something otherwise. It tells me that I need to do everything I can, on a daily basis to dominate my daily goals in order for my long-term ones to have a chance at survival. It's purposeful to have a long-term goal and a short-term goal, and they need to coincide with one another. I have a long-term goal to attract $5 million into that Roth IRA account that I spoke of earlier by the time I am forty-five years old. My daily goal is to stick to my budget that I set monthly. Will I reach this goal? We don't know yet. But I do know that I have everything I need to reach the monumental long-term goal: short-term goals around it, the behaviors set in place to establish this goal, and a purpose for having this goal.

One of the keys to my success is that I believe in what I'm doing unequivocally, without doubt. When I listen to people's stories and struggles, I find the majority of people have the exact issue. Most people genuinely have little to no belief in themselves, and this is why so many of our lives are in ruins.

One of the hardest things to do is to keep an open mind. I never think that what I know is enough. I am humble enough to admit that I know a whole lot of nothing. I may be an expert in a particular field based on what other people say, and that's a maybe, but to me there is no such thing as a guru or expert. I believe that we are all students, and that nobody is above us as students. The final key to what I do toward staying happy, productive, and motivated is to live in a space of consistent open-mindedness. Closed minds believe that they have the answer; they believe that they've seen enough, but a truly aware person accepts that he or she doesn't know anything. Once you choose to commit to being a student, you set yourself up to win, in just about every situation in life.

8 Things I Do to Stay Mentally Sharp and Productive

1. I allow my body to naturally wake itself up without an alarm clock, and I immediately drink water and stretch.
2. Clean my house, car, and mind consistently because clutter and disorganization do not need to be there.
3. A physical-fitness routine that involves stretching, weight training, cardiovascular activity, and the appropriate amount of sleep.
4. Set my intention for what I want the day to be like.
5. Create a plan for the day. My to-do list is never more than five things. I focus on doing five things per day to the best of my ability each day. Some days one thing may carry over to the next.
6. Define the purpose for my behaviors. I don't just go with the flow but ask, "Why am I doing this?"
7. Remind myself of my short-term goals, and figure out how I can impact them today.
8. Believing in myself no matter what other people think or say about who I am.

Creating Success

Creating success is about your mind-set; it's about if you've clearly defined your targets and if you truly understand the equation of action versus inaction. If you want to be successful in your marriage, in your career, in your fitness regimen, or in sports, you have to be willing to take more action than everyone else. You have to be willing to outwork yourself, even if you've already given your best effort. You must, at all times, be willing to learn something new, assuming that you will never be a master but always a humble student who is addicted to personal growth.

—Sylvester McNutt III

You Want to Be Successful?

"Go look in the mirror. Look at yourself, not with an eye of judgment, but just look. Look yourself in your eyes, like an enemy would. Look yourself in the eye like your lover would. See yourself as both energies. Again, without judging, because the only purpose here is to observe. Look at yourself, and ask yourself if you have what it takes, and again, don't answer or judge because that's not the mission here. Ask yourself the question after a deep spiritual stare into your soul, and once you hear what you need to hear from yourself—jump face first into the madness, and see what you can create for yourself."
—Sylvester McNutt III

"You live in a generation full of people who like to brag about their successes, and there is nothing wrong with that. But if you truly want anyone to care about your struggles too, never paint the picture that you are perfect; nobody can relate to perfection; we can only envy it. Paint the picture that you have cracks, but you're mostly strong. Creating armor like this, based in vulnerability, makes you magnetic and irresistible."

—Sylvester McNutt III, *Lust For Life*

"We have intricate skills and immaculate passions. Sometimes we are lucky enough to have a job that allows us to combine both: skills & passion. Sometimes we have to do something we are good at, even if we don't enjoy every aspect of it. My advice is to appreciate the skill set and the opportunity that you have. Your job may not be your "purpose," and it doesn't have to be; it can simply be something that you're good at doing that helps you take care of yourself, your family, and your desires in life. You can always do your "purpose" after work, on the weekends, or with your off time. Who says that you have to work a purpose daily?"

—Sylvester McNutt III, *Purpose*

"Closed minds believe that they have the answers; they believe that they've seen enough because they think they know everything, but a truly aware person accepts that he or she doesn't know anything."

—Sylvester McNutt III, *Awareness*

"Closed minds believe that they have the answers; they believe that they've seen enough because they think they know everything, but a truly aware person accepts that he or she doesn't know anything."

—Sylvester McNutt III, *Awareness*

Free your mind. Free your mind.
Free your mind. Free your mind.
Chase your passion. Chase your passion.
Chase your passion. Chase your passion.
Hone your skills. Hone your skills.
Hone your skills. Hone your skills.

—Sylvester McNutt III, *Lust For Life*

There are mental chains: **break them**
There are things you can't do: **do them**
There are places you haven't seen: **seem them**
Doubters: **let them doubt**
People: **let them talk**
Haters: **Hate**
You: **focus, work, and lust for life.**

—Sylvester McNutt III, *Lust For Life*

"Never allow your desire to be wealthy make you feel like you are greedy or as if you lack other morals. Being wealthy is great for you, the economy, and your family. If you want to be an innovative creator and wealth producer, go for it, and don't you allow anyone to tell you that you're greedy or selfish."

—Sylvester McNutt III, *Lust For Life*

"We have to stop feeling *shame* for our desire to achieve, for our desire to obtain wealth, for our desire to have access to whatever we want. Abundance is not limited to spiritual inner-peace or meditation alone; true abundance can be manifested into any pillar. If believe that you are worthy of abundance and you are willing to work for it, go get it, and never settle for less."

—Sylvester McNutt III, *Lust For Life*

"Where I come from, people do not believe that they are worthy of success, abundance, and wealth. Step one is to not think like the people who live where I come from. Step two is to not only think, but believe without any equivocations that you are worthy of abundance, success, and wealth."

—Sylvester McNutt III, *Lust For Life*

"Never allow anyone tell you that you deserve less when you know that you deserve more."

—Sylvester McNutt III, *Lust For Life*

"They're right, being rich isn't everything. Being a good person, with morals, and love is everything and I agree. However, having all of your bills paid, plenty of food, and the ability to live your life without financial worry is also everything."

—Sylvester McNutt III, *Lust For Life*

4: Taking Action Based on Your Purpose

In this moment, I want to tell you about my process as a writer and speaker. It's the same process I used when I worked in sales and played sports. I haven't changed the process and approach; I have only adapted it as life has changed for me. I must use the word "obsession" because I feel like without obsession and competition, you have nothing. Some people feel obsession is bad, and while they could be true, they also don't have best-selling books and don't live a life of abundance so I don't care about their opinion, at all. Obsession can have a place, it can be healthy, and it's needed to acquire abundance. In my mind, obsession can be a useful tool, depending on what the focus is. It's subjective. If we are obsessed with drinking alcohol, talking bad about ourselves, or even just coming to work late, these are obsessions that can ruin our lives. To me this is obvious. There are obsessions that need to be looked at with a second eye.

In my world, I am obsessed with the journey and never the destination. I'm obsessed with putting the work in, with learning from my mistakes, and going back to the drawing board to reinvent myself when I fail, which is often. I obsess about working and working smart. Some people like to use the phrase "work hard." I did my decades of working hard, and it served its purpose, but now I am into working smart. To me, that means using my time effectively, that means gathering new skills, and that means listening to my intuition when it tells me to. I don't fight my intuition at all. I go with it, and the reason I go with it is because I have failed so much in life that I trust it now. I have gone against it so much, I have observed so much, and I have been in so many situations that I have learned how to know when to trust myself. I believe that this process takes time, and that is why so many people do not trust their intuition. For example, in the process of writing this book, I had to take three months off, which is something that I have never done before with writing a book. Usually I just write straight through. I usually write every single day from day one until the book is finished. I no longer do that if my body or brain signals to me that I need a break. I've listened to my intuition, and it's telling me that I need to take breaks in between my writings. I cannot tell you why, but that is what my body tells me, so I listen. My goal with this book is to write at least three hundred pages of material. I believe that setting a goal for your obsessions is necessary. If you don't have an intended goal, your obsession will dominate it, and it will control you.

I love writing, but writing is an obsession, and I need to always feel like I am in control of it. The second that I feel like I no longer have control, I have to stop. This is why listening to intuition is so damn important. You cannot allow your job, your goals, or anything else to control your happiness via an obsession. Does this make sense? I hope so. The first thing that you have to do after you commit to practicing or working on your obsessions is you have to set a limit. If you're a basketball player, don't stay in the gym shooting for ten hours a day. Go in there with a target to make one thousand jump shots. Do you see the difference?

The lives we live now have a lot of components, so instead of spending time everywhere, set a target goal for that space. If you're working on your passion after work, guess what that means. It means you should not be doing overtime, you should not be wasting time at Starbucks socializing, and you should not be obsessively scrolling social media. It means that when you get off, you go directly to your obsession, so you can work on it because in that situation you don't have as much available time. A police officer whose obsession is bodybuilding should always have a gym bag with him or her. A writer who wants to write a book but works in corporate America should always have a notepad and a laptop around, so he or she can jot down ideas when they come, or write them in the notes section on your iPhone like I did until I escaped. We have already agreed that our obsession may not pay us, but it is our obsession because it makes us happy and gives us fulfillment. I'm not going to tell you to leave your job because everyone is not cut out to be a full-time entrepreneur. I am going to tell you to be prepared to spend time with your obsession. If you're a painter, you should have an easel and equipment in your car. If you play basketball, you should take your ball to class with you and dribble in the hallways between people as you walk to the next class. They'll tell you to stop dribbling, but fuck them; who are they? They're people who have decided to live in a box. Tell them this, "I want to be great, and in order for me to be great, I have to dribble this ball."

Disclaimer: Don't get yourself sent to detention because of this book. When I was working in corporate America, I took my computer with me to work every day, and when I had downtime, I would open it up and write poetry. My manager used to say, "What are you going to do with all of that? It doesn't pay you?" I said, "It doesn't pay you, but it definitely pays me because this is my safe haven. I'm writing for my own personal sanity and not because I'm looking to get paid. This job is crazy as hell, and the customer makes it even wilder, and so I find calm inside in the five minutes when I sit down to write my thoughts." See, I was obsessed with writing when I had a job that was paying me $75,000, which was good money in my mind at the time. Can we accept that our obsession does not have to pay us but that it can if we develop in that way? Obviously, I write for a living, and I quit my job to do this, so in my mind, we all can get paid for our obsessions. However, we have to be willing to go on the journey because it may take you thirty years to get a single dollar out of it; if you can go thirty years without getting a dollar, then you might be ready to chase your obsession.

Whenever the work obsession comes up, people always try to create this counterargument and use the word "balance." Fuck those people. And if you think like that, stop. Like I said, if you can create a healthy obsession and you can create limits for when you will and will not be in your obsession, then you can win. I am trying to get you to free your mind. I challenged you to do this at the start of this text: free your mind. I woke up today, when I felt like it, in a clean apartment with lots of food, got in a car that is paid for, and drove to a coffee shop when I felt like it on my time. I came here, ordered a hot chocolate, and a glass of water. I made four Snapchats about how I'm so proud of my progress in this book, and the sun is shining on me. The sun shinning is a metaphor for my life, it always feel good to be alive, to be me.

When my direct deposit went through over the weekend, it was enough to pay rent, to save some, and to book my trip to Costa Rica. So why in the hell would I worry about balance? My obsession has created the life that I have always wanted to live. I'm going to Costa Rica because of my thoughts, so tell me why I should focus on balance? I'll think about balance when I'm in Costa Rica sitting next to a volcano eating a mango. Fuck balance. You don't need balance; what you need is exactly what I said: an obsession with limits that you set. I promise you that I will go to Costa Rica, have someone take a picture of me eating a mango, and the caption will say "Fuck Balance". I promise you this. I am manifesting it right now because I deserve that experience. Are you understanding how *Lust For Life* works, do you get why I am telling you that I am going to do that? There is an abundance of everything in the universe, and there's a reason why most of us don't get it. It's because we have been conditioned by people who don't have access to the abundance to believe that we are not worthy or deserving of the abundance, and that's what fucks us up. We have to believe that we are worthy, that we are deserving, and it starts with our effort and our mind-set.

In conclusion, don't allow an obsession to run you because control is highly important. Set targets for where you will stop your effort, but make sure that you are practicing your craft. Lastly, the people around you are usually going to try to limit you, so don't get mad at them for it. Just accept that they see the world in a limited view, and you are expanding, you are in the mode of *Lust For Life*, they simply will not understand your energy until they read this book.

Action

It's seven thirty in the morning, and I am somewhere near the port in Juneau, Alaska, excited for room service to deliver my two bowls of cereal and a veggie omelet. I've been enjoying their freshly squeezed orange juice as well here. I feel compelled to talk to you about "action." We must understand action before we understand abundance because abundance is the art of attracting...via action. This is the first time in my life that I don't stress about money at all, and that time period has lasted for about the last five years. I don't say this to boast or to brag, but to make a point that abundance has a lot to do with two factors: one, the physical manifestation of your work, and two, the current mind-set that you have. The reason that I *feel* abundance, and it's important to note that abundance is a feeling and perspective, is because of the activity levels of previous actions. When I did not feel abundance in my life, it was because of my actions and my actions only.

A lot of people, gurus, and the motivational types speak on abundance as if there is a nine-step process behind it, and it's not that intricate to me. I want to be clear here because I want you to remember; I want you to take what you need from this text so you can implement it and that's why I see no need for smoke screens. I want to be clear that I am talking about the physical manifestation of goods, services, statuses, ideas, achievement, feelings, and anything that you personally are looking to achieve or reach—from an abundance standpoint. It's unfair of me to list what you want to hear or what I think you want to hear, you have to decide what it is you need. Abundance changes as we change. Remember that. In 2012 I was working in a job that didn't serve my desire and need to serve people, and I also felt trapped because making $70,000 just was not enough for me. You cannot make your desire or level of abundance based on other people. I hate books and programs that tell people how to be a millionaire or how to get this certain level of attainment because that's not authentic to me. Everyone does not necessarily need to be a millionaire.

Some of us just need to understand how to tell the universe what we want. Most of the time, we just need a little more of this and a little more of that, and for most of us then, we will feel like we are in a state of abundance. What is authentic to me, which is what I'm doing here, is to simply give the mind-set and stories behind the "how" and the "why." In the story I shared earlier, about why I needed to leave that job, I had two motivating factors, and they pushed me to create abundance. One was strictly based on the monetary value because I was not making enough, and the other was based on personal satisfaction because I was not serving enough people with my efforts.

You do not need to have ten motivating factors to desire abundance; one is just fine. If you have more, I believe that will give you more conviction and drive, but one is enough too. When you feel yourself desiring more abundance, it is imperative that you hone in on the motivating factor, and more importantly, you cannot shame yourself because of the desire. If you want to simply be more attractive so you can have more sex, there is nothing wrong with that goal. This means you might enhance your wardrobe, you may start eating more fruit, and you may hire a personal trainer. I'm not in the business of judging your goals or desires, I'm in the business of judging your mind-set behind the actions and then judging if the actions are aligned. This is the only thing I care about. If your goal is considered dark or taboo, that doesn't matter to me, and it certainly does not matter to the universe when you are in the place of seeker. You are a seeker. Your job is to determine what it is that is supposed to be sought and to seek it with an unshakable vigor. You are not here to play the morality game; if you do, you will tarnish the end result. Whenever you are in a state of desiring or proactively manifesting, the goal does not care about morality.

The goal cares about action. So instead of spending time overthinking wrong versus right, enough versus not enough, or if you're being greedy, just tell yourself exactly what you need to hear: "I am worthy, I am enough, I deserve this, and I will continue to put in the action to create this." If you do not proclaim that you are worthy, you will never be. If you do not tell yourself that you deserve it, society will tell you that you do not. Honestly, fuck this society because they want us to marginalize our thinking, our efforts, and they don't want us to get our piece of the pie. If there are people taking helicopters to work, doing yoga in Fiji, and getting the finest oven-roasted turkey breast in the land, why can't that be me? Why can't that be you?

Look, I love a turkey-breast sandwich with lettuce, tomatoes, and a really good spread on the bread. A really tasty turkey-breast sandwich is abundance to me. I tell myself that I deserve it often, because I do, and the sandwich is simply a placeholder for the equation that I've given you. You can substitute it with a car, with love, with status, with achievement, and so on. No matter what you want to substitute it for, you have to believe that you are deserving of it no matter how minute or how grand. If I have to work, pay taxes, and earn money to get resources in my country, why can't I have a bank account that looks like a phone number? If I'm going to be in a relationship, why can't I be with a woman who wants to have sex with me, who wants to make my life better, and who wants to see that she is a part of my happiness and not my depression? See, I've set a standard for myself, and it is based on my action.

Every action I take is to create more abundance. I have determined that I do not deserve to suffer at all, because what's the point in that? Plus, I've done that already, and it doesn't feel good. I don't need suffering or pain. Do you? Do you feel like you need to suffer? This is a question that you have to ask yourself—do you want to feel good and enjoy life, or do you want to suffer? These are choices that you have to make, but don't make the choice based on the fact that I told you my answer. You have to pick your own answer, and you have to really mean it. Like I said, don't compare your page five to my page eighty-five. I am at the point in my life where abundance is my only option. So what action can you take right now to create abundance in your life?

The first action that you can take, if I may make a suggestion, is to make a decision that has conviction and purpose behind it. Don't just make a goal about money or status, because that's what we are trained to do. You do not necessarily need money to have abundance; you don't. You can get by on a budget and have abundance. You can make a goal around fitness, around love, around personal happiness, or just the desire to learn more. Again, it's your life, but you have to decide, and you must have conviction behind the decisions, otherwise it's just a dream, and we hardly remember dreams. Nobody talks about dreams at funerals. People talk about two things and two things only at funerals: how a person made them feel and what that person did in their life. I'm about to mind-fuck you if you allow me; they are both the same thing. How you make someone feel is what you did and what you did is how you made them feel. You make people feel a particular way, and that is based on what you feel on the inside, so do you feel abundant, or do you feel scarce, unworthy, unloved, and undeserving? When I meet people and when I leave my conversation and interactions people feel reenergized; they feel loved, they feel valued, and they feel like they're important. I feel all of that about me, and so this is the energy that I carry. What type of energy and impact are you carrying right now? Are you carrying abundance or suffering? So my question to you is this: Are you taking the actions necessary to create, to manifest, and to sustain abundance in your life? If the answer is no, then you have to ask yourself what you're willing to do today to make it happen. What actions are you willing to take?

You Need to Learn Indifference

Consider this to be the first section of black magic. In our society we love to shame other people who think in ways that are different from us; we love to shame ideas that don't seem to have morality that the general public agrees with, and we outcast people who bring true introspection and thought to topics. I reject this society; it doesn't make much sense, and since you're reading *Lust for Life*, it is clear that there are pillars that you're rejecting too. We already talked about the things that you care about; we referred to them as your obsessions, and it's safe to say that caring takes a lot of energy. Wouldn't you agree? You need to learn indifference, which means that you genuinely don't care about the results of some outcomes, regardless of whether they are in or against your favor. Let's go deeper. Psychology has noted that we have something called human-channel capacity, and that is our ability to process information inside a particular category. If we have many things that we care about, like our identity, our goals, our finances, our health, our relationships, our families, and our growth as a human, isn't it safe to say that caring about those things requires a lot of energy? Since caring uses so much of our channel capacity, our ability to process information in a particular category, isn't it safe to say that there are some things that we simply will not have the energy for? My argument is that there are *more* things that we need to put into that category that we do not care about. Not because we hate the world but because we love ourselves, and we do not have the ability to spread our energy effectively among all these different pillars. We need to care less about certain things, especially if these things cause us stress, dysfunction, and depression. If these things bring us pain, disharmony, and stagnation, why should we keep them? The most logical human being cannot logically give me an argument for why we should keep these activities around that break us, especially if we do not have to. Do we have a choice? Do I have a choice to do a job that I enjoy, or do I need to work at the job that pays more, even though it brings me a great deal of stress? This is why indifference is needed. I make myself suffer at a job because I have tricked myself into thinking that there is a particular lifestyle or income that I need. This is what fucks us up and the way we free ourselves is to effectively introduce indifference. It seems like, in my situation here, I am unhappy with my job because it causes me a great deal of stress. Based on what

we have talked about so far in this book, I am
allowed to make a choice, because all I have is
behavior and information. The information at
hand is that I am stressed out, and stress kills your
immune system, and makes your life shorter.
Since I am a logical thinking being, my logic tells
me that I need to consider changing my job or my
perception of my job. Since I cannot change the
perception of my job because the stress is real, my
only option is to change my job. I cannot change
my job because my bills are too high, and this is
the point where most people feel stuck. They do
not become indifferent about the things that they
pay for. For me, I look at it like this: Fuck this
television; I'm selling it. Fuck this car; I'll walk.
Fuck this bed; I'll sleep on the floor. Fuck Netflix;
I'll read. Fuck partying and drinks; I'll drink
water. That is total indifference about the lifestyle,
and until you are willing to sacrifice, you will
never rid yourself of the causes of stress. You have
to be willing to say, "Fuck this; I do not need it; it
is not serving me." The main reason we struggle
with letting go is because we care too much about
the wrong things or the wrong people, at the
wrong time. We have been conditioned to care too
much about things that cause us pain or keep us in
a state of suffering; think about that. We are
trained to care about the news, but please tell me,
have you ever in your life seen a positive story on
the news? Sports are exempt because that's not

news; that's entertainment. The news is filled with nothing but depressing stories, and yet we watch it every single day. Why? I'm sorry; why the fuck do we watch the news? Is it because we are conditioned to accept programming that feels like death and depression? They talk about how someone was murdered, and we don't even flinch. We should be freaking out when we hear about death, about mental illness, about government officials arguing and potentially putting us in another world war, but we don't even flinch because we are numb. I don't watch the news. I refuse to accept that conditioning because it's too painful for me. I am an empathetic person, and I care deeply about many things. My mom says, "Well, how do you find out about world events if you refuse to watch the news?" I said, "I do get world news, my world. I focus on my inner world, because if a war occurs in there, I have to be ready to create a cease-fire. If there's a mental-health issue in there, I have to be ready for that journey. So I do watch the news, just not the external news." She smirked, shook her head, and walked away. I would love to care about every bombing, about every murder, about every politician who steals money, about every school that has a shooting (like mine did in 2008), about every other problem that the world encounters, but that is not fair to me at all. It's not fair to you either. You can use this analogy for just about anything really. Like rap beef. I love hip-hop music, and it seems like every week a new rapper is beefing with a new rapper. I don't care, and I don't follow that type of stuff; my channel capacity just does not have space for it; does yours? Do you follow your favorite celebrities' personal lives? Question: Do you follow your friends' personal lives too? If so, how? Could you be a better friend if you got out of these celebrities' lives and minded your business first and your friends' second? My favorite basketball player is Russell Westbrook, and has been since about 2011 when I watched him play live in Phoenix, Arizona. Do I follow his life outside of what he does on the basketball court? No, and I never will, unless I meet him, and we genuinely become friends. My obsessions are writing, eating, learning, spending time with people I care about, and not stalking people like Russell Westbrook. I am not saying, "do not follow people you like". I am saying do not waste hours and hours stalking them and diving into their news when you should be focused on your own. It's not an effective use of my time or yours. I am indifferent to caring about celebrities, news, and anything that takes away from my obsessions. Do we understand what is going on here? We are conditioned to be distracted, to lack focus, to lack purpose, to lack direction. I would never ask you about a five-year plan, because obsessing about the future is nothing but a state of suffering.

However, there are practical thoughts that make sense regarding the future. Most people cannot even articulate their goals, their passions, or what they want to get out of this moment in life. Most people do not have any direction nor do they understand their sense of belonging. I can simply answer this question because I am not distracted, I am not focused on irrelevant ideals or practices, and I am focused on my obsessions. In the book, *Lust For Life*, I want you to introspect your life. I want you to pay attention to what you pay attention to and ask yourself, "Is it worth my time? Is this content making me richer?" This book is giving you life; it is making your life better, and it will be a tool in your progression because you love to be engaged in deep thought and reflection. So as I close this section, I have one question for you: What can you get rid of today that will help you focus on your obsessions and passions? Please forgive me; I lied. I have one more question, and you can answer both of these below; I'll leave a little space. How much better would your life be if you stopped caring about some of the irrelevant things you care about? Answer below, so you can come back to this later, and consider writing about what you will and will not focus on.

"I am a fan of the journey. I am a fan of the process. I am a fan of taking nothing and turning it into something. I am a fan of working toward the things that I claim I want while being patient. I am a fan of trusting the process."

—Sylvester McNutt III, *Process*

"There is an abundance of everything in the universe, and there's a reason why most of us don't get it. It's because we have been conditioned by people who don't have access to the abundance to believe that we are not worthy or deserving of the abundance. We have to believe that we are worthy, that we are deserving, and it starts with our belief and only happens once we take action."

—Sylvester McNutt III, *Abundance*

"Don't let someone with a limited view of life box you into his or her small perception of how things could be. Odds are, the person is afraid to live, afraid to die, and afraid to take a risk because he or she doesn't want to lose. If you want to be great or want to create, you have to leap out on faith. You have to be willing to take a loss in order to win big. If you're not willing to do anything, then you are not ready to attract everything."

—Sylvester McNutt III, *Don't Let Them Box You In*

"Believe that you are worthy, and watch blessings come into your life at a high rate. Believe that you are not, and you'll watch every blessing come and go without you ever grasping on to the ones that are truly meant for you. Life is truly about the perspective that you decide to take on."

—Sylvester McNutt III, *Manifesting*

Until you are willing to sacrifice everything that you have, you will never rid yourself of the causes of stress. You have to be willing to say, "Fuck this; I do not need it; it is not serving me, and since it is only hurting my life, I must learn to live without it."

—Sylvester McNutt III, *Sacrifices*

"Look around. There is an abundance of everything: love, money, opportunity, financial stability, mental stability, and happiness. If you look at that list and feel like you're missing something, don't obsess about manifesting it. Pause, breathe, and then ask yourself if you deserve this abundance. Once you feel the answer is yes, only then will the universe start rewarding you."

—Sylvester McNutt, *Abundance*

"The main reason we struggle with letting go is because we care too much about the wrong things or the wrong people, at the wrong time."

– Sylvester McNutt III, *Lust For Life*

"People leave. People stay. You can't control either one. Be grateful for those who stay and the lessons that you learn from the ones who go."

– Sylvester McNutt III, *Lust For Life*

"Nothing lasts forever, nothing stays the same, the fall is our reminder that everything must change. In life, you either learn how to adapt to change or you suffer because you expect it to always be as it once was. New things are born, and old things die, either way you have to adjust to survive."

– Sylvester McNutt III, *Lust For Life*

"Closure is an internal process, no external person can give it to you. If you want closure accept reality and stop living inside of your fantasies."

– Sylvester McNutt III, *Lust For Life*

I don't watch the news. I refuse to accept that negative and poisonous conditioning because it's too painful for me. I am an empathetic person, and I care deeply about many things. My mom says, "Well, how do you find out about world events if you refuse to watch the news?" I said, "I do get world news, my world. I focus on my inner world, because if a war occurs in there, I have to be ready to create a cease-fire. If there's a mental-health issue in there, I have to be ready for that journey. So I do watch the news, just not the external news."

– Sylvester McNutt III, *Lust For Life*

"I run from anything that attempts to destroy my inner-world. These external forces no longer have the power to control my peace or my happiness, I have the power."

– Sylvester McNutt III, *Lust For Life*

I want you to pay attention to what you pay attention to and ask yourself, "Is it worth my time? Time is something that you should never waste because once it is gone, it is gone forever."

– Sylvester McNutt III, *Lust For Life*

5: What Does It Mean to Deserve Abundance?

Poetry is fun; in fact, it gives us the ability to look at words in a nonliteral way. "Poets have been saying that you deserve abundance for decades," I have said it too, but what does that really mean? If a person knew how or why he or she deserved abundance, don't you think he or she would have gone after it? And that's the power of poetry; observe this with me: *you deserve abundance and peace and love, and a life that is worthwhile.* That sounds wonderful as a post on Instagram and will get me ten thousand likes, but how is that twenty-two-year-old in New York who has depression, no money, no education, and no skill supposed to believe that?

What I just presented you is my writing style in a nutshell. Yes, I am poetic. I am a poet, but I have to go deeper than what feels good because I want to understand the process of how and why. I need to know the psychology, the sociology, the science, the reason, and the motivation. I'm here to understand and to, at least, explore all of that. I feel that is a common bond that you and I have. You the reader, me the writer, and us the group of humans who are looking to explore ideas have found each other, so we can explore together. I don't want to give you advice or tell you what you deserve; it's not up to me, but if you'll allow me, I will tell you about my life. I want to share a story with you that will help me explain this to you, and when I say this, I mean what it means to deserve abundance.

I'm sitting at Sip Coffee, a local brewery and coffee shop in Scottsdale, Arizona. I'm wearing sweat pants and a long-sleeved black shirt. I didn't put on any underwear this morning when I woke up. I didn't care to. I'm drinking green tea. I feel good; I feel alive. I have a basketball game tonight at seven o'clock, and I can't wait to play my favorite sport. For breakfast, I had an egg sandwich. I put some tomatoes, spinach, onion, and cheese in the eggs as they were being made. I also ate a Cara cara orange with the sandwich. Daisy ate with me; I think she broke her foot, which is why she's at the doctor's office, and I'm writing this to you. I'm listening to "The Line" by DVSN. The previous song was "The Morning" by the Weeknd. Those are two of my favorite songs.

I have no concerns, no ailments, no drama, no stress, and no problems. I am not mad at anyone; I do not feel a certain way toward anyone who is negative or pessimistic. The wind blows every few seconds or so; it's Arizona, so the wind does not blow much. Every single time the wind blows, I stop typing. I don't think about the words. I simply look up into the sky, which has no clouds, and I gaze at nothing. I look off into the distance and let my eyes shift as they may. It feels right. There is no thinking, no confusion. I'm not worried about how these people in the store are judging my outfit or presence, they almost do not exist to me, even though I am aware of their presence. I'm not sure how many people are in this building. I am in my bubble; I am in my space; I am focused on absolutely nothing. I am in the moment, simply allowing the moment to grab me and allowing the words on this page to flow as they come.

I do not want them to be perfect; what is perfect? There is no such thing as perfection. I had twelve dollars in my wallet, and now I have nine. My tea cost three dollars. I just looked up, and three beautiful women were in my sight. Hold on; let me appreciate the view, and I'll be back with a thought, whatever that thought is. Actually, I'll be back much later because Daisy just texted me. "Come get me." She was getting x-rays on her foot that I'm confident is broken. When we return to the page, I'll tell you why I shared this deep dive into my present moment and state of mind; it matters, and if you can remember every little detail about what I said, you will understand abundance on a far deeper level than any human being you've met or will meet.

Two weeks went by before I had a chance to revisit this writing, and I'm glad. I'm currently on an airplane headed to Vancouver, Canada, and I remember why I needed to write you that last passage. When you are truly in alignment with yourself, with the energy around you, and with your purpose, you feel like everything goes in a natural order. I was looking out of the window staring at the clouds, the ground underneath me, and when you do these types of activities, you can usually activate a deep level of daydreaming. I heavily encourage daydreaming because it leads to organic inspiration. Have you ever gotten a bright idea in the shower? That's because you're so calm; the temperature of the water relaxes you, and it allows you to be creative. Creativity gets sparked through environment and observation, not force. As I'm looking at this incredible moment, completely immersed in the now, it dawned on me that I needed to revisit you because we have an unfinished topic.

Here's why observing the present moment is the only thing you should really focus on: when you stay completely in the moment, you allow creativity to rise to its highest level. When you stay in the present moment, you allow the pain from yesterday to disappear because you realize that it holds no relevance in this present moment. When you stay truly in the moment, you give yourself abundance because that is how you realized that you have enough. I was sitting at my favorite coffeehouse with only nine dollars in my pocket that day. Was that a lot of money in the grand scheme of life? Probably not, but was it enough for me to get a sandwich and some tea? Of course it was, and in that moment, that was all I could've desired at all. On top of what I had, I gave myself good vibrations because I listened to songs that made me feel good. I was doing an activity that gave me pleasure and made me feel good. I did this because I knew that I deserved abundance.

I notice in our generation that there are people who are winning, and they don't even realize that they're winning because they're comparing their victories to others. You can't compare your page one to someone else's page eighty. That's disrespectful to your journey and to theirs. Doing this does not give you abundance; it robs you of it every single time. Personally, I have five books that have been in consistent rotation since 2013. I'm only five books in. I have sold at least one book every day in that time frame. There is an artist or writer now reading my book, looking for inspiration to live solely off his or her art like I do, and what do you think he or she will do to himself or herself if he or she compares his or her day today to mine? We haven't put in the same work. I've written two thousand words or more every day since 2002. I went to college to learn how to write and speak, to study speakers, went to seminars, quit my job for writing, and have built my little empire off the consistent grind of creating new content. You can't compare yourself to me because you don't deserve this level of abundance based on the duration in the craft. I've simply put more work in than you. Now what happens to my perception of my success when I compare myself to people who I like such as Tony Robbins or Eckhart Tolle? Eckhart has one book that has sold ten million times, and he has had at least ten episodes on Oprah. What happens when I compare myself to a speaker like Tony Robbins? He puts 6,000–9,000 people in a room to hear him speak, and I put 150–200 in a room to hear me speak. Am I not successful? Do I not have abundance? What about the fact that Tony has been doing speaking for thirty years and I've been doing it for four? This is why I will never compare myself to him. I don't deserve his level of success right now, because I haven't put that kind of work in. Now, one day I'll put 6,000 people in a room, but that's not today, and I have to be OK with that.

We have to accept that we are all on a journey. None of this is easy; it requires a lot of hard work and sacrifice, and most importantly, it requires you to be patient. Tony, Eckhart, and Sylvester all started at zero. No matter where the numbers are now, no matter how we judge success, and no matter where we want to go, we all started at zero. Don't tell me that you want to be a

New York Times best-selling author if you don't
truly put the work into your craft and skill to earn
that. Of course, some would say that goal setting
increases your ability to achieve, and that's
nonsense to me. Goal setting toward a behavior
that is set toward action is the only way you will
ever be successful. It is the only way you will ever
create abundance. In other words, don't chase the
goals; chase behaviors. Many people
underestimate the amount of action that it will
take to create, to manifest, and to hold abundance.
Grant Cardone wrote a book called *The 10X Rule*,
and he says that no matter how much action that
you think you need, you will need to make ten
times that amount of action to actually reach your
goals.

"I heavily encourage daydreaming because it leads to organic inspiration. Allow your mind to drift. Free your mind."

— Sylvester McNutt III, *Lust For Life*

"I'll network with anyone. I'll build with anyone. However, You have to work hard, you have to believe that anything is possible, and you cannot be shady."

– Sylvester McNutt III, *Lust For Life*

"We have to accept that we are all on a journey. None of this is easy; it requires a lot of hard work and sacrifice, and most importantly, it requires you to be patient."

– Sylvester McNutt III, *Lust For Life*

"Making money, attracting abundance, and living the life that you desire is only about how many people you help. Stop thinking about yourself, and start thinking about how you can impact others if you want to attract a high level of abundance."

—Sylvester McNutt III, *Lust For Life*

"Life does not have to be black and white. It does not have to be this or that. Sometimes, you have to live in the gray area. Sit back, and just observe everything without picking a side. There is a lot of power in allowing things to be as they are without forcing your will on the outcome."

—Sylvester McNutt III, Lust For Life

"The actions that you take determine everything: your love life, your bank account, your level of personal satisfaction, and your ability to attract abundance. If life is not what you want it to be right now, take a look at your behaviors objectively. Whatever needs to go, release it, so you can hold on to the type of life that you deserve."

—Sylvester McNutt, Lust For Life

There is no such thing as "I know already."
To attract abundance you have to assume
you know nothing; you must be open to all
information even if you feel it is wrong. You
must be a being who is free of ego and
judgment of all things until you understand
them. Never seek to see if something is
right or wrong, only seek to understand it.

—Sylvester McNutt III, *Lust For Life*

"Getting what you want out of life requires you to listen to your emotions and to ignore them. You must master this skill; otherwise, it will master you."

—Sylvester McNutt III, *Lust For Life*

"In life, you will encounter people who have bad energy, bad attitudes, and energy that will drain you. There will be some days when you will have the energy to pick them up, but this is not your job or your duty. Stay in your lane. Focus on your inner world. Pick yourself up, and those who are naturally ready to rise will; the others will not."

—Sylvester McNutt III, *Lust For Life*

"It is not your responsibility to try to turn other people's bad energy into good energy, that is their job, and you cannot afford to always spend your energy that way. Focus on your inner world; you cannot control the external one."

—Sylvester McNutt III, *Lust For Life*

"In order to truly be successful at any point in your life you have to be willing to forego one of these and sometimes all: sleep, sex, alcohol, friends partying, fitting in, making sense, drugs, acceptance from others, reason, logic, hate, love, and inner barriers. It will be hard, but life after you learn how to make sacrifices will be easy."

—Sylvester McNutt III, *Lust For Life*

"To attract abundance, you must release the judgment that you have of others. The only thing worth judging is if you are or are not taking enough action to create what you want."

—Sylvester McNutt III, *Lust For Life*

"You cannot afford to spend time being mad, upset, petty or unruly. There is no peace or harmony in these states. Forgive. Let go. Use your energy to be productive, to rise yourself. Release the emotions that aid your downfall."

—Sylvester McNutt III, *Lust For Life*

"You need abundance, and there is no reason to believe anything else. It's perfectly normal to want to have a bank account that looks like a phone number, a lover who wants to fuck you, and a life that feels like a party on a Friday night."

—Sylvester McNutt III, *Lust For Life*

"Everything does not have to be a big deal. In fact, most things are irrelevant and unimportant. Your desire is to feel good, to look good, and to have a good life, so when irrelevant things happen, do not make a big deal about them. Let it go, quickly. Let them go forever because wasted time does nothing for you other than bring you closer to death."

—Sylvester McNutt III, *Lust For Life*

"There is a law of abundance that you must observe if you want to have an abundance of happiness and joy. This means that at all times you must believe there is an abundance of opportunity and resources for you to get. You're a passionate, calculated, and intense human being. You don't need to care about everything. Choose your energy, and focus wisely, so you can always focus on creating the right vibe that is followed by massive action."

—Sylvester McNutt III, *Lust For Life*

"Care deeply about what matters, observe the rest."

– Sylvester McNutt III

"Never stoop down to a low vibrational level: don't argue, don't get petty. You should try to bring them up to your level and if you can't, move forward, it's not your fault that you need to leave them behind."

– Sylvester McNutt III, *Lust For Life*

"Love should feel abundant.
Get rid of anyone who wants
you to believe otherwise."

– Sylvester McNutt III

"Look at your partner,
text them something sweet.
When they look at their phone,
kiss them on the cheek."

– Sylvester McNutt III

"If you really understand love, then all you want to do is give it and receive it as much as possible."

– Sylvester McNutt III

"Never guilt your partner, just hug them, and let them know it will be okay."

– Sylvester McNutt III

6: Exploring the Concept of Love

Can we explore love further? Do we really know what it is? Can we reject what we have been taught by society, by church, by parents, by media, or by other people's relationships so we can really understand the depths of what love really is? Can we reject what the movies have given us about love only for us to come to our own truth? Let's explore; let's introspect; is it possible that we truly do not understand what love really is? Everyone talks about finding love; is that possible? Can you find love, and if you could find it, if there was a formula, wouldn't it be better known? What does it mean to find love? How do you find love? I've found money lying on the ground before. I picked it up. I put it in my pocket. Can you do love like that? Is it something physical that you can just find? We can certainly agree that love cannot be found in the physical, tangible sense. So then that leads us to this question—if love cannot be found in a physical form, why do we expect people to be loving, to love us, to give us love? I'm not asking because that desire is wrong; I'm asking you because nobody else is going to make us think deeply about this. Can we open some rabbit holes?

Let's go deeper. **When you think of love what are you exactly thinking of?** Is your perception of love a relationship with another person? Is love the way you see the world? Is love a feeling? Is love a state of consciousness? This matters. Exploring this matters. You do, at all times, need to be fully aware of how you view love. You may have idealistic views, and these views may cause you a great deal of suffering. Odds are, if you're an American woman, then you do have idealistic views of love, of dating, or how things should be. In fact, this is why so many women suffer. *I'm coming from this angle with empathy, compassion, and inquisitiveness because I want to understand.* In my travels I hear the American woman compare the present moment to how it should be; this is idealistic. This is a direct form of suffering. To create the separation from what is to what it should be is conflict. If you're an American man, odds are you haven't explored what love is because you're not allowed to via socialization, because you've been told that it's not masculine, because it's what women are supposed to do *allegedly*.

Men suffer with love, largely, because they are told that they are not worthy or that they should not focus on it. Men are told to focus on other motives like the chase of financial freedom, but is that chase of money really love, especially if we've already explored that love is not a physical good? There is no authority, no teacher, no guru, no leader, nor a blueprint that can truly testify to what love *should be*. Here, we are simply exploring these thoughts; we are exploring what it means; we are exploring our viewpoints because we don't want to suffer. That is the point here, so don't let me, the writer, act as if I am the authority. I am not. You are. How deep do you want to go with this? Are you willing to accept that your ideals cause you suffering, and are you willing to accept that your perception of what love is causes you the depression, the sadness, the anxiety, the angst, and the unsettledness that you deal with? Is it possible that you don't truly understand love, and if that's the case, could this realization actually cause you to grab a deeper level of understanding? I hope so.

Let's explore attachment. Remember; we are rejecting everything that we have been told in order to explore this. We are rejecting the church, the parental guidelines, and the media. Is there an element of attachment that comes with love? Is it necessary? What does this attachment mean? We must explore this. Why? We deserve to be mentally free, and we deserve to operate on a plane of consciousness that rids us of all suffering and pain.

Why do people feel like they own their spouse, their lover? This is weird to me. There is a certain amount of possessiveness that comes with our relationships; have you noticed that? The expectation that you won't have *inappropriate* conversations with the opposite sex—who determines what's inappropriate? Is it possible that what you may feel is inappropriate is different from what your husband or wife may feel is inappropriate? Is it possible? And then what happens when these conversations happen? The other person feels betrayed; he or she feels like you're less trustworthy or like you are a malicious person. Does that or does not that feel like a form of control? Since when did this almighty love that we speak of create these elements of control? Let's go deeper; let's go much deeper. If you're in love, how come you're only happy when the other person does things for you that makes you happy. If they give you pleasure, like sex, food, or compliments, then you are happy and in love. If they give those same things to another person, all of a sudden, you are not in love. You are angry. They shouldn't be giving food, sex, or compliments to others because in your mind that's not love because that's how you've been trained to think. Explore this because the exploration of this idea literally might free you from the mental chains that society, your parents, and the media have placed upon you. Is it possible to love more than one person? Is it possible to show love to one person and then to another? Where does the control come from, the jealousy, and the obsessive desire to make sure that you are the only one receiving the benefits of another? Where does this controlling nature come from? Is that love? That can't be love; what do you think? Is that love to you?

Let's talk about where this comes from. It comes from a need to have security. This makes sense if you take a step back and think about it all, in its entirety. We are inherently selfish, especially those of us who have grown up with the western-world mind-set. We are entitled, we are deserving, and we are selfish. The need for security rules us. We want those compliments only to be intended for us. We want sex, which is pleasure for us, to only be given to us; we want resources like food and shelter to only be given to us. Somehow we've accepted that this is love and that nobody else should receive any of these benefits that we are worthy of. So if our partner offers an iota of these resources to another person, then he or she does not love us. This is the extreme logic we live with. If a person who claims to love us offers these benefits to another person, then we must act irrational, throw a fit, and act in a way that will cause him or her not to give *our* benefits away. This is the conditioning that many of us live with, and my question to you is this: Does this make sense? Consciously, does this make sense, or does it bring you suffering? Does it bring you happiness? There is a demand and desire to feel safe in relationships, and this desire is causing us to feel sadness, attachment, and entitlement, so how can that be love?

In order for us to move away from the attachment, the entitlement, and the sorrow that comes from this need for security, we must understand that love and relationships are not the same. We must understand that love is a feeling, a state of consciousness, and an emotion. Sometimes people can express love through their actions, through their words, but for the most part, it is an intrinsic occurrence. Love is something that happens inside of you. Expecting to control, to manipulate, or to motivate others to fit your idea of love will always cause you suffering. They may comply, but they will fit into their form sooner or later. You will be met with the choice to accept them as they are or to try to doctor them up to fit your perception. If love is an intrinsically occurring event, what is a relationship, and why do we associate them? This is a great question, and it is an important one. If you say sixty-thousand words per day, how many of those words are "I love you"? If you have one hundred thousand thoughts per day, how many of those words are "I love you"? In both cases it's probably less than 1 percent of the total. Does this mean that you don't love them? No, you do, but it's not something you think about or express every single second of every single day. Please continue to explore this with me; this writing is here to give us freedom, joy, and internal bliss.

So what is a relationship? A relationship is an interaction between two people. There are many different levels to which a relationship can exist. Sometimes it may be often. Sometimes it may be daily. In some cases it may occur once every six months. Some relationships—and right now we are not talking about romance; we are simply describing the nature of relationships— some relationships are set up where value or energy goes back and forth between the two parties. In some relationships, like in the example of tutor and student, one person is doing a great deal of giving where the other person is doing a great deal of receiving to the other person for his or her benefit. Every relationship offers value; there's something you can learn from every interaction that you have.

In some relationships there is an element of love, and this is what we need to explore. We need to explore what people mean when they say things like "I want to fall in love" or "I want to find love." At this point we should've completely addressed all the questions, thoughts, and situations presented internally. If you have a notebook, consider going back and taking notes. Understanding these questions and everything that I present here will literally free your mind. You have never lived in total freedom. You have never lived in a space of not wanting, not needing, not seeking, of total bliss of this moment—I'm sure of it. If you have, you would not be reading this book; you'd be off somewhere in a place where no one could reach you. Once you have truly experienced true freedom, you'd stay there as often as practically possible. It's important that you not breeze by this material in a matter of hours. This material here is not presented as entertainment; this is the backbone of this book. The beginning of this book is truly about shining the brightest light internally at yourself. Go look in your bathroom. You see that big mirror that aids your vanity every single morning? This book is that mirror, but it's all around you, and instead of only reflecting your world appearance, this book's aim is to literally dissect what you think internally, how you process things internally.

Why am I doing this? The better question is, why are you reading this? Well, it's easy. We feel as if we want to be totally free. With this freedom we think that a deeper version of love can permeate, or maybe we think that real love, whatever that is, will somehow find us. If that is your purpose for reading, and if that is my purpose for writing, then I guess only time will tell. Honestly, I cannot tell you my true intent as the writer right now because I truly do not know. I only know, that in this moment, I have been given a light to spread thought on the exploration of love, on the concept "This Is What Real Love Feels Like." I haven't forgotten where we are. We are going to explore why we say things like "I want to fall in love" or "I want to find love."

If you don't agree with this first sentence, gather up enough open-mindedness to bear through the entire paragraph, but here it is: **love is an emotion.** Some may agree. Some may disagree. At the root of what love is, love is an emotion, and I'm sure most would agree with that. Even if you cannot truly agree, you can at least see that love is an emotion. I hope you can because we are about to go much deeper. Let's do what poets do, and let's add a layer to this, so it feels like something we see on television or social media: **love is the most powerful emotion a person can feel.** *How does that feel?* That probably feels more familiar to you, especially if you have grown up in America like I have. We can play with that type of saying or anything like that; it honestly makes sense for this book. It's beautiful poetry. If love is a powerful emotion, isn't it safe to say and isn't it easily agreeable that emotions may cause and do usually cause certain behaviors? If I was deathly hungry and didn't have any money, wouldn't it make sense for me to steal a loaf of bread from the corner store that throws them away if they're not sold by a particular date? You may not like the word "steal," but if you were in the situation and you felt deathly ill from your hunger, I assure you that your morality police hat would come off, and your survival kit would kick in. You would steal. You would eat the bread. You wouldn't have a guilty conscience about it. You wouldn't because it felt right to you in the moment. What about anger? Anger is an emotion, right? Usually anger can cause people to act in a violent way, whether that is physical violence or just verbal abuse, and violence can and usually does occur after anger. Is that something we can agree with, and do we see the connection? The emotion, anger, caused the action of violence. So what about what we are exploring here today, the concept of chasing love, the concept that we want to find love, this idea that we want to fall in love? Love is an emotion, like anger, or as in the bread example, it is an emotion like desire. When you're hungry and you want that bread, it is a state of desire that persuades you to steal it, is it not? So logically, if we say, we want to fall in love, couldn't one also say we want to fall in anger? Obviously, nobody would really say that, but my question is, is it possible? I can see clear as day that I can fall in love or anger. Obviously, love feels better, so we say things about our need to fall in love. Anger is another emotion that we experience as humans, but we don't say we want to fall in that; why? That is the most important question of the day, and once you explore this with me, it may change everything you think about love. Here I'll tell you why, and then you can decide if it works for you.

Falling in love is not sustainable. Love is simply an emotion. No matter what adjective a poet, a man, a woman, a priest, or a church places before love, it is simply an emotion. Emotions are temporary states. So even the poet who proclaimed the emotion of love cannot stay around all day, because it is just an emotion, meaning, all emotions come and go—period. This is a fact of what an emotion is. If you have experienced any emotion, you can see this. The emotion of love does create behaviors of love. Behaviors based in love are what keep the connection going. Never obsess about falling in love; instead focus on the behaviors that will help you show love over and over again.

Behaviors like feeding another person, like complimenting someone for his or her effort, or giving someone a hug are all behaviors that show love.

Can we accept that falling in love in not sustainable and really shouldn't be our goal? Can we accept that if our goal is to be in a relationship with someone that feels like love, that love will come and go? Can we accept that you can have a relationship and love and that the more love you have in the relationship, then the more sustainable the relationship is, because of love?

I travel the world talking to people about dating and relationships, and I can honestly tell you that an overwhelming majority of us just talk about our idealistic views of love.

After we've read this chapter, it's safe to say that none of you will do that going forward. We can have relationships with love, with the powerful love that causes men to write poems, and the love that has women crying on pillowcases. Sorry; I had to be dramatic there. Ladies, stop crying on pillowcases please. So the answer is, yes, we do understand and accept that falling in love is only love, no matter how great it may be. We do accept that a relationship is only a relationship, and it may or may not have love in it. These are two independently occurring entities, one an emotion and the other a choice.

So let's explore this: how do we get love, how do we feel love, how do we show love, how do we take that in and put it into the choice of a relationship? Love is a feeling; it is not a choice; the relationship is a choice, so how do we get the automatic emotion to help us in the relationship? That is what we must explore now. Take a break. Breathe. Digest.

Is it possible that we can attract this thing that poets call "real love," and if so, how? How do we get love, how do we feel love, how do we show love, how do we take that in put it into the choice of a relationship? Love is a feeling; it is not a choice; the relationship is a choice, so how do we get the automatic emotion to help us in the relationship?

We concluded that there is a distinct difference between love and the concept of being in a relationship, and the distinction is what I would call separation. Separation is the first key that we need to measure because without understanding separation, we cannot truly understand love.

"People always ask me how I feel about getting back with an ex. And honestly, it's a confusing question because it's not a black or white answer. Part of me feels like once there is love there, then there is always love, and building off of true love is always a beautiful story. The biggest factor is if the behaviors have changed, the ones that ended the relationship. If there is still love there, both people are willing to make it work, and the dysfunction has been destroyed go for it. However, if I have learned to live without you it's hard for me to go back."

—Sylvester McNutt III, *Lust for Life*

"You were absent from my life. I learned to live without you. It will be almost impossible for me to let you back into my life."

- Sylvester McNutt III. *Lust For Life*

"Some people have successfully gotten back with their exes. I am not some people."

- Sylvester McNutt III, Lust For Life

"Teach them how to work through a tough time, but if they don't have it in them, don't suffer trying to keep someone who doesn't want to be kept."

- Sylvester McNutt III, *Lust For Life*

"Respect your exes. You shared time. You shared energy. Have respect for them. Don't talk about them like you didn't choose to be in their presence daily."

- Sylvester McNutt III, *Lust For Life*

"Don't let an ex play the, let's try it again game just because you're actually moving on. Stand strong."

- Sylvester McNutt III, *Lust For Life*

"Being friends with your ex can be a healthy bond, but you have to both be moved on from the dating part of the relationship to make the friendship work."

- Sylvester McNutt III, *Lust For Life*

"If kids are involved, don't beef with your ex in front of them. They are watching. Show them that you can communicate with the devil without having bad energy."

- Sylvester McNutt III, *Lust For Life*

"Don't make the kids suffer because you two could not reconcile your differences. You should both want the same thing: the kids feeling loved, accepted, and like they have support from two mature parents."

- Sylvester McNutt III, *Lust For Life*

"You have kids with them. Don't talk bad about them to the kids. Be objective. Explain what's going on to the kids. Be reasonable and never think that your children are *too young* to know the truth. They're watching. They're listening."

- Sylvester McNutt III, *Lust For Life*

"If you're single never obsess about trying to create a relationship with another person. Focus on the relationship that you have with yourself: build it up, figure out who you really are, and find ways to love yourself more. This relationship is the precursor for how all other relationships will go. "

—Sylvester McNutt III, *Lust for Life*

"Being single means that you don't have to worry about any games, nobody is cheating on you, and you're at home in your bed with no worries — enjoy it. "

—Sylvester McNutt III, *Lust for Life*

"You're single: Focus on your savings account. Stay off the dating apps. Hydrate. Do yoga. Chase sunsets and Lust For Life."

—Sylvester McNutt III, *Lust for Life*

"If you're single and you're looking to find someone who is worth your time, all you need to do is do activities that you enjoy. Meet someone organically, that way. "

—Sylvester McNutt III, *Lust for Life*

Single Person Manifesto,

Being single does not mean that something is wrong with you, it is not a curse. Being single does not mean that you are actively trying to date every single person that you see. Being single does not mean that you are jaded, heartbroken, or unwilling to meet new people. Single people are not required to actively search for partners; there is nothing wrong with being single and no person would shame a single person for their choice. A single person is allowed to go on dates without pressure to push their life to a committed relationship. If a person just wants to have fun, go on dates, and live their life as they see fit then they are allowed to. As long as a person is honest with themselves and the people they interact with, there is no harm and no foul.

—Sylvester McNutt III, *Lust for Life*

"Alone for the moment until you find someone to be with forever."

—Sylvester McNutt III

"There is no authority, no teacher, no guru, no leader, nor a blueprint that can truly testify to what love *should be*. Love is one of the few things that can never be explained, it can only truly be experienced."

—Sylvester McNutt III, *Lust for Life*

"We deserve to be mentally free, and we deserve to operate on a plane of consciousness that rids us of all suffering and pain. We deserve to love in a way that heals and never hurts, us or them."

—Sylvester McNutt III, *Lust for Life*

"Never seek to control, to manipulate, or to marginalize your lover. True love is about growth and expansion."

—Sylvester McNutt III, *Lust for Life*

"Being in a relationship is not hard. A relationship is basically doing these three activities over and over: eating, sleep, and talking."

—Sylvester McNutt III, *Lust for Life*

"Being in a relationship is not hard. It is much easier if you just be yourself. It is much easier if you find a person who genuinely aligns with you. It is much easier if you communicate what you think and how you feel. it is much easier if you accept each other because a relationship that lasts has two partners who accept each other's differences."

—Sylvester McNutt III, *Lust for Life*

"Show me how to love you.
Tell me what you need.
Tell me when I do what you like.
If you're silent I won't know so be loud
and proud. Teach me how to love you."

—Sylvester McNutt III, *Lust for Life*

"Tell me your favorite meal so I can make it for you. Tell me how to hold you so you never feel alone. Tell me your biggest secrets so I can so you that I'm trustworthy. Tell me what you need so I can give you everything that you want."

—Sylvester McNutt III, *Lust for Life*

"I am not in a hurry to fall in love, I am in a hurry to get to know the real you so that I may love you."

—Sylvester McNutt III, *Lust for Life*

"I don't need a million friends because I'd rather have one lover who I can do a million different things with."

—Sylvester McNutt III, *Lust for Life*

"I want to love you in a way that heals you, I hope it feels like heaven. I will remove any pain from you, anything that feels like hell."

—Sylvester McNutt III, *Lust for Life*

"I knew I struck gold when I found someone who was worth waking up to. That's the hardest thing to do. Finding someone to go to sleep with is easy."

—Sylvester McNutt III, *Lust for Life*

"I never expect perfect, so don't act like a counterfeit. Give me the real you so I know who I'm dealing with. I need the authentic you no matter how deep, no matter how dark, no matter how strange."

—Sylvester McNutt III, *Lust for Life*

"Don't be in a hurry to fall in love just because you love love, you will disappoint yourself if you're not patient and understanding. Instead, take your time to study your partner. You need to master the art of observation, without judging your partner, without trying to change the little things that you don't like. Real love is about acceptance so take your time learning them, be patient with them, and never fear asking questions that will help you understand them on a deeper level."

—Sylvester McNutt III, *Lust for Life*

"Never obsess about chasing love. Chase goals. Chase dreams. Chase the behaviors that are going to make you better. You don't chase love; you allow that to find you by accident, and when it finds you on accident, you'll know that is was supposed to find you purposely."

—Sylvester McNutt III, *Lust for Life*

"Falling in love is great, but showing someone you love them consistently is even better."

—Sylvester McNutt III, *Lust for Life*

"Falling in love is not a choice, staying in love is."

—Sylvester McNutt III, *Lust for Life*

"Love is a behavior to me as well. Show me that you love me don't just tell me. Love is more than just a feeling, it is an action, it is a lifestyle."

—Sylvester McNutt III, *Lust for Life*

"Love is a feeling; it is not a choice; the relationship is a choice. Their love for you is unconscious, and they can't control it. Whether they treat you well or poorly is a reflection of themselves at that moment."

—Sylvester McNutt III, *Lust for Life*

"Sometimes we have been broken from our previous relationships, and we lose hope that a new relationship will bring that thing that we call "real love." Truth: a poor, bad, or toxic situation from your past does not have the ability to control the chances of you falling in love in the future. Love is magic; it happens when it's supposed to, every time. What happened has already occurred, so don't allow it to block you from these blessings that are meant for you."

—Sylvester McNutt III, *Lust for Life*

"Don't push away the beautiful
people who are trying to pull you in,
people who are really trying to love
you for you, even the ugly parts."

—Sylvester McNutt III, *Lust for Life*

"Love is freeing, it supports a person where society has chosen to break him or her. Love is rage; it causes the recipient to lose himself or herself, causing paralysis of the mind even though everything feels miraculous in the heart."

—Sylvester McNutt III, *Lust for Life*

"If you want love, don't look outside for it in another person. Other people don't give you love; they give you words, actions, and nonverbal cues to their subconscious. How you interpret what they do is how you view "love." So to find it, look at your perspectives of what it is and what it is not."

—Sylvester McNutt III, *Lust for Life*

"Often times, we expect another person to love in the way that we do. That's not how love works. We must study our partner. We must learn how they like to give and how they like to receive love, that's real love."

—Sylvester McNutt III, *Lust for Life*

"The tough part is when the relationship makes you feel like you want out, but the love seems to be keeping you in. Be patient, and try to lift each other up without holding each other down. All real relationships will go through hard times, don't quit just because it's hard, that's what cowards do."

—Sylvester McNutt III, *Lust for Life*

"It's so important that you communicate what you want and what you need. How is another person supposed to love you if you don't communicate these things? The truest form of this experience happens when we can be completely naked with our vulnerabilities and totally immersed in the magic of our expressions. The freeing type of love, the love that creates healthy relationships, basks in the energy of vulnerability and being forward. Put out there what you want and need, so the universe and your lover can reward you."

—Sylvester McNutt III, *Lust for Life*

"I never want to control my lover, ever. I want her to feel like she is free to do what she wants even if I don't like it. I want the same freedom to come to me, and well, it's because love doesn't mean control or entitlement. Love means that I want to take care of you, because I have a deep allure for you. If she can look me in the eye and say "I love you," then that means she has looked inside of herself to know that this journey won't always be pretty. I want to love her, and I never want to control her. I want to be loved and never want to be controlled either. Love is free."

—Sylvester McNutt III, *Lust for Life*

"I just figured out how to free myself. This also helps me feel free inside the relationships I have. I accept that they don't owe me anything at all, and everything that they choose to share is a gift. Their time is a gift; their effort is a gift, and every single time they put me first, that is a gift that I should cherish. We could say the same thing for what I give, but it's not about my ego at all. It's about how I view love, and I want to view love as an expression that is freeing and liberating. I want to forever live in gratitude when they offer me a gift, and this has totally freed me."

—Sylvester McNutt III, *Lust for Life*

"They keep telling us to take things slowly, but once you taste the touch of love, all you want to do is overdose on the smells, the sounds, and the feelings as fast as a heartbeat will allow."

—Sylvester McNutt III, *Lust for Life*

"Pour a glass of wine, grab a deck of cards, and connect with your lover over genuine conversation. Quality time is one of the easiest ways to build, to improve, and to maintain a beautiful connection."

—Sylvester McNutt III, *Lust for Life*

"You don't need someone who completes you today. You need someone who accepts you completely forever."

—Sylvester McNutt III, *Lust for Life*

"Never let anyone play with your feelings,
you deserve more than that. If they cannot
communicate, clearly, then save yourself
and find the one who can fulfill the basics."

—Sylvester McNutt III, *Lust for Life*

"You're the type of lover who always fights for your partner. You just need the type of lover who is going to stay and fight with you, no matter how tough it gets. You know what you want when you want it so you need someone who wants to choose you over and over."

—Sylvester McNutt III, Lust for Life

"Tell me about your past so I can learn your history. Tell me about you are today so I may accept you. Stay by my side so I can show you real love forever."

—Sylvester McNutt III, *Lust for Life*

"No matter what, be patient with this entire game called love. You don't need to find people who know how to say I love you. You need to find people who will show you that they love you, people who actually know how to value another human being."

—Sylvester McNutt III, *Lust for Life*

"No matter what, be patient with this entire game called love. Games that are played too fast often result in loss or failure. Any athlete knows that you have to let the game come to you; you have to take what is presented to you when the time is right. You have to master patience because you never want to settle with someone who feels wrong."

—Sylvester McNutt III, *Lust for Life*

"No matter what, be patient with this entire game called love. If it is for you it will flow, if it is not it will feel forced. Pay attention."

—Sylvester McNutt III, *Lust for Life*

"No matter what, be patient with this entire game called love. There are many people who are addicted to the idea of love. You don't need to have one of them fall for you because they won't catch you if you don't match their ideals."

—Sylvester McNutt III, *Lust for Life*

"No matter what, be patient with this entire game called love. Some people like to bend the rules for their benefit, those are the ones who will break you. Be patient so they won't mistake you for someone who is replaceable."

—Sylvester McNutt III, *Lust for Life*

"No matter what, be patient with this entire game called love. Nothing of value shows up when you want it right away, however, it will show you when you need it. If it's valuable you'll have to earn it, you'll have to fight for it more after you've caught it too."

—Sylvester McNutt III, *Lust for Life*

"Starting a relationship might be hard for you because you're reserved, because you don't let too many people get close to you. If you feel like your introversion is preventing you from finding love, try your best to step outside of your routine. Some people simply do not find dates, lovers, and friends because they never leave the house."

—Sylvester McNutt III, *Lust for Life*

"Here's the crazy thing about being an introvert and wanting to find love. You have to actually talk to people, even though, in your natural state you'd rather be alone. However, you're a hopeful romantic, so you don't actually want to be alone."

—Sylvester McNutt III, *Lust for Life*

"You're an introvert but you want companionship. Never break yourself in the process of trying to find someone but be ready to break certain habits if they're stopping you from attracting the love that you deserve."

—Sylvester McNutt III, *Lust for Life*

"As an introvert, you would rather stay in the house, and interact with yourself or the people that you already know. There is nothing wrong with that, however, two things depend on your ability to network: your intimate relationships and your income. Keep the contact information of many people because you never know who may have a financial opportunity for you. If you can, engage in conversations with people until you reach your extroversion limit, because some of those conversations could lead you to true love. Don't feel like you have to trap yourself in the house because you're an introvert but also don't feel like you need to be everyone's friend, because that's not you. Know your limits and trust the process."

—Sylvester McNutt III, *Lust for Life*

"You're an introvert but you want companionship. Never isolate yourself to the point of illusion. You do not want to lose touch with reality simply because you've boxed yourself into a mental cage."

—Sylvester McNutt III, *Lust for Life*

"Two people who have built an unbreakable connection, the type of connection that always attracts them back to each other is rare. When it feels like you're separating and falling apart, but the love is so real that it always bring you back. That's beyond real love. Keep it if you have it."

—Sylvester McNutt III, *Lust for Life*

"The most dangerous thing you can do in a relationship is ignore the person that you love. Nobody wants to be shut out, nobody wants to look stupid. Listen to your partner, even if you don't want to at that moment. Listening is a form of love, never forget that."

—Sylvester McNutt III, *Lust for Life*

"One of the hardest things to do is explain your feelings, while you're feeling them to someone who may not understand. Everyone has a person from their past who has called them crazy, stupid, or made them feel like their feelings had no place. Never be that type of person for your lover, instead, listen deeply. Listening is love. Give your partner reassurance that their feelings can always be shared with you."

—Sylvester McNutt III, *Lust for Life*

"Relationships do not always last, in fact most of them are not forever. The scars, the memories, and the lessons that you learn, well, those will last forever."

—Sylvester McNutt III, *Lust for Life*

"You're waiting for someone who understands pain & love like you, someone who is deep and complex, someone who simply wants to love. You're waiting for the lover who treats you right, the one who never makes you feel wrong or crazy."

—Sylvester McNutt III, *Lust for Life*

My heart has a deep appreciation for those "let me know once you've when you made it home" type of people. You're basically saying that I'll be on your mind until you know that I'm okay, wow, that's real love.

—Sylvester McNutt III, *Lust for Life*

"You love in such a deep way that you should never settle for just anybody, just to say that you have somebody. Your love is rare, it heals, and it uplifts people when they feel broken or down. Find the person who is your other half, the person who makes you feel like you are whole. Find the person who loves just as hard as you, the one who will not make you look stupid for being loyal to them."

—Sylvester McNutt III, *Lust for Life*

"I never want to go on another date where the other person thinks it's okay to play on their phones the whole time. I'm not boring & I'm not fighting for attention. If your timeline is more important, then you are not the right lover for me. I don't care about finding gossip or small talk on a date. I want to get lost inside of your soul. I want to trek though your mind, & engage in deep conversation with you. I'm old school. Get off the phone and look me in the eyes, let me know that you're real, show me how bad you want it."

—Sylvester McNutt III, *Lust for Life*

7: **Separation and Oneness**

Separation is the root of all conflict; it is the root of war, and it is the very reason why we have so much hate and dysfunction in our world. It is easy to kill someone if you see them as something or someone outside of you, if you label him or her as a threat or the enemy, but how does he or she get to that point? At some point, some government, some entity, some church, someone, or you have labeled him or her as a threat, an enemy, as dangerous, or as incompatible. Because of this, you kill; there is war, and do not think we are using "kill" in the literal sense alone here because it can represent more than just that. We can talk about how you kill friendships and connections with people because they share different religions, race, or socioeconomic status. We kill people who are, allegedly different from us, in the name of what? Just the difference? I do not have the answer; I do not have your answer; I only have the questions needed to go deeper here.

Let's go there together, and let's explore this together. If you label me as the writer, as the leader, or as the expert, what happens? You force yourself to be a novice; you force yourself to take my opinion, and you rob yourself of the truth. Never do that. There is no such thing as an expert, never. We are both students; we are both discovering this together, and we are both exploring the topic because without the exploration of it, we will continue to separate ourselves from everyone, which will continue the madness that we live in.

It's safe to say that we kill things, in the figurative or literal sense that we feel is opposed to us. We have war with societies that are different from our own over opinions that are different from ours. Yes, there have been civil wars, occurring in the same countries, but those wars did indeed have opposing parties in the same country. War, in the physical sense of guns, airplanes, and militia is no different from emotional warfare, war at home, war in the workplace, or war on your social-media time lines. This is all the same. It is all connected.

Disliking someone because of his or her ethnicity is war; disliking a gender is war, and being upset because a man and a man or a woman and a woman want to be together is war. So this brings us here; why? In all the examples mentioned, there is a level of separation. In every single example that you can think of, there is conflict between sides. If you go watch a basketball game, one team wears white and the other team wears a colored jersey; why? It's to indicate that one team is going against the other, in an effort to win, and this is why we all suffer.

We all find reasons to think that we are wearing different jerseys, when in fact, none of us have jerseys. Everything that we use to separate ourselves is really made up. The country you were born in is literally just an island, but somehow because of the flag and the food you feel as if you belong, which isn't bad. We are not labeling things as good or bad; we are simply just exploring, so we can understand ourselves and the world. So we develop a sense of pride, which is ego; we develop this nationalism, and it tells us to speak loudly about our country and how great it is.

For me personally, I live in America, and if America were a person, he or she would be that arrogant jock in high school whom nobody likes but everyone pays attention to because he or she is attractive, powerful, and assertive. America is attractive, but America has deep-seated issues with depression, insecurity, self-hate, self-destruction, and self-love. You follow this analogy, right? I am using my country because I do not want to use yours, to disrespect yours, but I am comfortable with talking about mine, and then you can relate it to your country, or you can simply observe the prose here.

So here we are full of pride; full of ego; full of nationalism and love for our flag, fight songs, national anthem, bill of rights, and our ego that tells us that we are the best country. Please see that the country analogy can be broken down to any level of life. It can be broken down to your ethnicity, to your socioeconomic class, or to your education level. So my question is this: Is a sense of pride and nationalism necessary and required? Is it possible that we can appreciate each other's country without saying that one is better than the other? Is that possible? If so, couldn't that mind-set abolish war, the physical war that takes lives and the mental war that keeps us all trapped? Is it possible?

What if one country is better than the other because of the conflict going on in one country or the opportunity that another has to offer, would that mean that another country is better in that regard?

This is a great question. When we say that something is better than the other, what we are doing is forming an analysis of comparison. Now, it's up to you if you want to be objective or subjective with this analysis. To be objective means you are looking at the facts only; to be subjective means you are adding in your personal biases; neither is wrong, but both have some sort of value. If you're raising a family, looking for organic food and schools that will provide the particular education that you desire, then you are of course being subjective and saying that one country is better than the other makes sense. But here's the deal: you can get a great education at the University of London, and you can get a great education at the University of Southern California. Two different countries, but is one really better? That is really up to you to determine, but when you do so, don't say that one is better than the other, because then you diminish what the other has. Instead, say that one gives you more value at this time than the other. It's very possible that you could get an undergraduate degree from the University of London and a postgraduate degree from the University of Southern California. Follow me here; both those experiences could be considered a different experience, but in your book of life, it would be one experience. This is one experience for you, one unified experience, and there really is no need to separate them at all.

Before I was a full-time writer, I was a personal trainer, and before that I was in sales management. Different titles, of course, but really it's all the same conglomerate experience. Personally, I choose to look at the learning factors, the benefits, and what I loved about each situation. Why? I don't want to suffer, and what if I have to go back? You do yourself a great disservice if you devalue an experience and then have to experience it again, and that is another root of suffering. Why do you delve into it? Because you have been taught to compare experiences, you have been taught to separate experiences, instead of just looking at them as one continuous pillar, as one continues to exist.

I just thought of a great example to help explain separation, and this will actually allow us to dive into oneness. This book, Lust For Life, will be my sixth book. When this book comes out, I guarantee that someone will ask me, "Sylvester, what is your favorite book?" At this point, I have a choice, a perspective to pick. I can pick the book that made me the most money. I can pick the book that was the most rewarding to write. I can pick the book that made my love life better. I can pick the book that has the best cover. I can pick this book because it will be the newest book, and I'd like to sell as many copies of the newest book as possible; I have options. Or, I can choose to see it as *one* big book, one continuous journey, and that there really are not six books at all. It's just one career, one flowing entity of consciousness, of thought, of love, and of expression. Why pick one book, which is a loaded question, when I can appreciate and love each and every one of the books?

Oneness

To accept oneness is to literally free yourself of the strength of your ego; it is to free yourself from unnecessary fighting that will happen in your future, and it is to free yourself from stress that you will have. Oneness is the art of accepting that you are connected to all parts of the universe. It is to accept that you are already whole, that you are unified, and that you are complete. Please read this with an open mind. Suspend the thoughts that you have about yourself. Please do not label yourself as not enough of this or not enough of that. This is simply about the concept of oneness, so please join me in the introspection of this idea, and you can find your truth as it makes sense to you; is that fair for you?

Science is the art of finding the truth via inspection, via testing, via observation, and it is supposed to, at all times, be free of religion, personal biases, financial coercion, and error. This is what science is at its core. If a theory becomes a scientific fact, it does not mean that it is excluded from all introspection. No matter what you believe to be the truth today, please accept that you are also allowed to introspect and to find new truths. Odds are you've been given a *truth* from your nationalism, from your parents, from your media, from your teachers, so is that really truth? Reject the truth that others have given you because that is not truth; that is lazy and is disrespectful to your journey. You have been given a life of separation. You check your bank account, and you attach some type of personal worth to it. You look at your followers online, and you assume that you are more or less than someone who has more or less. You feel cooler if you have more, and you feel inadequate if you have less—who taught you this? If you're a popular girl in high school, you don't hang out with or talk to the unpopular and unlucky girls because they're *not on your level*. If you're the star football player, you hang out with other jocks. Hanging out with someone from the debate team is awkward for you. These status symbols add value to your ego and to your self-esteem, and again, I am not shaming anyone here. I am simply painting a picture by using the common generalizations that we can all understand or have at least observed. Think about the employee who has moved up the corporate ladder, and now the person holds a management position, an upper-management position at that. Because of the title, the person feels like he or she is more in control, he or she loves to bark orders and give directions, and most importantly, his or her ability to be coached or trained decreases because he or she feels like he or she is the big dog in the house now. The person feels he or she has the biggest bite, the loudest bark, and also feels he or she can do no harm.

"Separation is the root of all conflict; it is the root of war; it is the very reason why we have so much hate and dysfunction in our world. We feel like we are separate from everyone, from the world, from ourselves even. We box each other into demographics: black, white, asian, women, middle class, wealthy , etc. This little boxes keep us from seeing the big picture, thy keep us at odds with each other when we're truly all even."

—Sylvester McNutt III, *Lust for Life*

"Disliking someone because of his or her ethnicity is an act of war on the human race. You should dislike someone once they prove to you that they are a threat, that they bring pain, or show you that they intend to do ill will upon you. Disliking someone because of their skin is utterly stupid. You're allowed to have your narrow-minded view if you'f like, but please, do not pass it to anymore children. For the sake of our children, let's allow our children to decide what they want and how they want to be."

—Sylvester McNutt III, *Lust for Life*

"In order to create a relationship that can never be broken, both people must agree that the entire goal is to create oneness. Oneness is the idea that it's you and me, me and you, and that we are connected in all aspects. Oneness is the idea that we are together, we are a unit, and no matter what we will never give up on each other."

—Sylvester McNutt III, *Lust for Life*

"In order to create a relationship that can never be broken, both people must agree that the entire goal is to create oneness. Oneness allows you to deal with the dark messes that relationships may bring, and it turns them into an omnipotent beautiful light."

—Sylvester McNutt III, *Lust for Life*

"In order to create a relationship that can never be broken, both people must agree that the entire goal is to create oneness. Oneness tells each partner that when they do start to feel like they are breaking, the bond is so strong, that the other person will always try to put them together."

—Sylvester McNutt III, *Lust for Life*

"In order to create a relationship that can never be broken, both people must agree that the entire goal is to create oneness. Oneness turns the sad nights of tears into mornings of rough sex, laughter, and smiles."

—Sylvester McNutt III, *Lust for Life*

"In order to create a relationship that can never be broken, both people must agree that the entire goal is to create oneness. Both people have to agree to protect each other from all outside forces so the connection will remain unbreakable on the inside."

—Sylvester McNutt III, *Lust for Life*

"Part of the reason we have so much trouble in the world is because we feel we are so disconnected from everyone and everything. You genuinely are connected to everything that you experience. Nature is not outside of you, the humans who you interact with are not outside of you, and the truth is that everything is connected to you."

—Sylvester McNutt III, *Lust for Life*

"To accept oneness is to literally free yourself of the strength of your ego; it is to free yourself from unnecessary fighting that will happen in your future, and it is to free yourself from stress that you will have. Oneness is the art of accepting that you are connected to all parts of the universe. It is to accept that you are already whole, that you are unified, and that you are complete."

—Sylvester McNutt III, *Lust for Life*

"Reject the truth that others have given
you. To accept their truth without
discovering your own is to blatantly
disrespect your journey with a bald face lie.
You have been given a life of separation.
You check your bank account, and you
attach some type of personal worth to it.
You look at your followers online, and you
assume that you are more or less than
someone who has more or less. You feel
cooler if you have more, and you feel
inadequate if you have less; who taught you
this? When are you going to look inside and
find the real truth about who you are?"

—Sylvester McNutt III, *Lust for Life*

You have to own it: the debt, the problems, the stress, the confusion, the feeling of being lost or misunderstood. You have to own every single ounce of it, so you can change it.

If you feel the problems are not yours or as if they are outside of you, then you will suffer. You have to win every single ounce of it, and only after you are accountable for your problems can you make a change. The universe is calling for you to accept that you are indeed one with all of your problems. Once you blame yourself for all of your problems you will actually free yourself. You will finally have power to create, the power to choose, the power to make different choices.

—Sylvester McNutt, *Lust for Life*

"This is your reminder: Free Your Mind"

—Sylvester McNutt III, *Lust for Life*

"It's simple for you. You want to feel good, you want to look good, and you want to have an abundance of love in your life. Perfect; don't for one-second think that this is something outside of you and that it is unattainable. You must feel as if you're deserving of this right now because you are."

—Sylvester McNutt III, *Lust for Life*

8: How to Be Ego-Free

"Discovering this changed my life: It was the moment I accepted that no matter what I thought about who I was or what I had, nobody owed me a damn thing. Ego gets in the way; it creates entitlement. I know that nothing is owed to me."

—Sylvester McNutt III, *Lust for Life*

"It's not easy to climb big hills, so if that is your current path, you must apply an unreal level of patience. Some missions in life are impossible today, but that doesn't mean it'll be impossible forever. Don't let your ego keep you on a task if it's time to fold it in and move on, but don't quit too soon if you haven't been patient enough.

—Sylvester McNutt III, *Lust for Life*

"My process to reduce my ego while creating consistent happiness and love is simple: I let go of the things that don't matter, and I hold on to the things that do."

—Sylvester McNutt III, *Lust for Life*

"It's so important that we learn the art of apologizing and accountability. There are too many adults who revert back to victim complex and excuses. And then, they do not realize that the process of bliss and happiness requires you to be accountable for your actions. At times, we feel like apologizing may make us weak, but that is our ego talking. Never allow your ego to stop you from healing relationships."

—Sylvester McNutt III, *Lust for Life*

"This is your reminder: nobody owes you anything, nothing will be given to you, and you will have to sacrifice to get everything that you want."

—Sylvester McNutt III, *Lust for Life*

"A lot of human beings struggle with forgiving themselves for their mistakes in life. Taking this angle forces you to be blind to your progress, potential love, and wealth. You must forgive yourself for your mistakes. Forgive. Let go."

—Sylvester McNutt III, *Lust for Life*

"Don't give up on your dreams because everyone else is giving up on theirs. Don't think that you cannot be successful because unsuccessful people look at you like you're the same as them. Don't quit when things get hard just because you're used to be around quitters and they've normalized it. You're not normal, get wild, and go for what you want."

—Sylvester McNutt III, *Lust for Life*

"Until you learn how to say "It was my fault, and I made a bad decision" without guilt-tripping yourself or feeling bad, you will suffer. Most people will read that statement as a pitiful victim complex, and it will cause them to feel down. People who live in a space of **abundance** and **love** view that statement as a declaration of power and ownership. The accountability fuels them and gives their life the power needed to take control. Same words, different meaning. The choice is yours."

—Sylvester McNutt III, *Lust for Life*

"Every single person in the human race feels stupid at one point or another; there is no reason to get down on yourself about your journey. Making mistakes, saying the wrong thing, and being naïve are a part of the experience. Don't make it harder than it has to be by beating yourself up with words when you should be using them to protect yourself."

—Sylvester McNutt III, *Lust for Life*

"We hold positions in arguments because we feel there is value in being right. The wave of consciousness that is about to sweep the globe involves people who understand that nobody has to be right. We can both free our ego, free the position of being right, and simply choose to hear each other's perspective. We can choose to hear each other, to empathize with one another, and to work out peaceful solutions."

—Sylvester McNutt III, *Lust for Life*

To free your ego, say these things to yourself every day over and over: Nobody owes me anything. I only deserve what I work for. I am important, but I am not the center of the universe, however, I am the center of my universe. My life will advance once I learn how to tangle my universe with others, consistently.

—Sylvester McNutt III, *Lust for Life*

"People can have an opposite or different thought from mine, and we both can be right, while neither one of us is wrong. This can happen at the same time. It's called listening to understand and aligning with others."

– Sylvester McNutt III, Duality

"The wise person in the room is the one who tries to see every person's perspective, every angle, and every possibility. This person knows that his or her perception is narrow, small, and limited, so he or she always remains open to other possibilities. This person chooses to engage in dialogue that uplifts the mood and brings in new information. The wisest person is after the pursuit of dialogue, the chase for information, and never attempts to sit on a throne like they're above these pursuits."

—Sylvester McNutt III, *Lust for Life*

"Expectations should be an intrinsic thing; there's not much you should expect of anyone. It'll just lead to disappointment, more confusion, and a lack of total acceptance."

—Sylvester McNutt III, *Lust for Life*

"I don't expect anyone to stay loyal to me, to have my back, to fight for me. I expect myself to do that for myself at all times - I got me."

- Sylvester McNutt III, *Lust For Life*

When you abolish your ego, you start asking people "How are you doing, and how can I help you?" more often than you worry about yourself.

If you listen to most people, they're always talking about themselves and their drama, and they waste precious hours whining about a lack of abundance.

Never be that person. If you want to win, impact people. Call them when nobody else does. Text them when nobody else does. Show up at the games that their parents don't go to. Listen to the poems that they're scared to show the world. Listen to them when the world tells them to shut up.

Figure out how you can serve the next person, and this will not only abolish your ego but it will also uplift everyone around you, which in turn uplifts you.

—Sylvester McNutt III, *Lust for Life*

"If you genuinely care about someone, then offering him or her your ego as a partner will always be a failure. You should desire to offer him or her a partner who doesn't care to be right but one who cares to seek the truth. You should offer him or her an ear and a heart versus a cold stare and an empty hug. You should offer him or her companionship and understanding over judgment and guile. A partner who is ego-free is the best kind of lover to spend time with. The person doesn't look at love as what he or she can get but as what he or she can give."

—Sylvester McNutt III, *Lust for Life*

when you understand love you stop looking for what you can get and you focus on what you can give. you stop creating pain for others and you create pleasure and healing.

– Sylvester McNutt III, *Lust For Life*

To be ego-free always remember that you just have to pay attention to how many times you say the words "I" or "me." If you find yourself talking about yourself, your wants, and your needs all the time, then you may be speaking from a place of ego.

If other people are involved, replace I with "we," "us," "let's," "together," "ours," and "as a team."

—Sylvester McNutt III, *Lust for Life*

"When you're down and out, don't ever assume that life is over, that you you'll never be able to bounce back, or that it's you against the world. I can't lie to you and tell you that the road to recovery will be pretty or easy; you're right; it's going to be a very hard process. Do not forget to smile, not for anyone else but for yourself. You're still alive. You're still breathing. You still have another opportunity to turn this entire ship around. It's now or never; it's up to you and nobody else; your time to create a legendary story is right now. What will you do with this energy?"

—Sylvester McNutt III, *Lust for Life*

"Your ego is this fragile being that lives inside you, and sometimes it causes you to be extrasensitive to situations that you should overlook. It causes you to get wild and unruly when you should remain calm and steady. Your ego causes you to scream about what you are or how you should be treated, when you should be silent and observant. That ego, the one who lives inside of you causes you to hold grudges and creates uncalled-for emotions that do nothing but seek and destroy your appeal to consistent happiness."

—Sylvester McNutt III, *Lust for Life*

9: Free Your Genius

"I believe that every human being has genius-level potential, but reaching that level requires patience, practice, and an obsession towards learning. A true genius is a person who loves growing, a person who loves exploring ideas, and a person who doesn't fear the possibility of being wrong."

—Sylvester McNutt III, *Lust for Life*

"This society has many components. Some of these pillars do their best to help you, to motivate you, and to inspire you. Some only know how to be an adversary, an enemy, and a dominating force that tries to destroy you. Your best bet is to realize that all the power is inside you, and you should never leave it up to society."

—Sylvester McNutt III, *Lust for Life*

"A genius is a person who has an exceptional intellectual or creative power. We grow up watching superheroes as if they possess skills that we do not. Don't ever limit your genius because other people have limitations on what you can do. You can move mountains, you can stop time, you can heal, and you can fly. Believing this or not is only about your perception. The difference between true success and failure is one's perception."

—Sylvester McNutt III, *Lust for Life*

"Self-doubt comes from two things. One, you're comparing yourself to someone else or to another part of your journey. Two, you're believing the narrative that others have written for you about what you're capable of."

—Sylvester McNutt III, *Lust for Life*

"Geniuses move in silence while their actions make a lot of noise.
Don't tell anyone anything until it's time to show them everything."

—Sylvester McNutt III, *Lust for Life*

"Sometimes your position in life will cause you to use me, just know that I will be using you back. We can both benefit from each other, just bring something to the table so we can both eat. We can create a win-win situation, and when it's over, we can both walk away with our dignity since we knew we were just using each other."

—Sylvester McNutt III, *Lust for Life*

"The best marketing for anything is word of mouth, not your own mouth, allow others to do the talking for you."

—Sylvester McNutt III, *Lust for Life*

"The goal is to win, by any means, so if you have to change your role, your beliefs, or your team, consider doing that. Don't let other people trick you into thinking that their perception of loyalty is the only thing that matters. Some people believe in blind loyalty. At the end of the day, I have to be loyal to my dreams and goals. In that process I have to cut some people off, change teams, move, and do everything I can to grow into the winner that I deserve to be."

—Sylvester McNutt III, *Lust for Life*

"I believe in loyalty, I don't believe in blind loyalty to any person or any entity. If your actions hurt me I am going to switch up where my loyalty lies because I don't remain loyal to pain, I refuse."

—Sylvester McNutt III, *Lust for Life*

"Everyone doesn't need access to you. Some people are draining and they don't even know it. You're allowed to say no, you're allowed to not answer calls, you're allowed to break plans, and if you need to save yourself do it."

—Sylvester McNutt III, *Lust for Life*

"A wise person understands that most people are easily triggered emotionally. Knowing this, the wise person learns how to do two things: control his or her emotions, and control the emotions of others."

—Sylvester McNutt III, *Lust for Life*

"Control your emotions or other people will learn how to control you by pitting you against yourself. Everything doesn't deserve a reaction. Relax. Breathe."

—Sylvester McNutt III, *Lust for Life*

"You have to let go of all of the sad things if you want to hold on to happy ones. You have to let go of negative people who drain you if you want a positive life that is full of energy."

—Sylvester McNutt III, *Lust for Life*

"One of the keys to inner-peace is to understand that everything doesn't deserve an emotional response. You can observe, you can understand, and you can move on without getting bent out of shape or acting irrationally because of your emotions."

—Sylvester McNutt III, *Lust for Life*

"Observe more. Understand more. Emotions are not facts, they are internal reflections of moments. Breathe more. Stop letting people control you because you haven't figured out how to control your emotions."

—Sylvester McNutt III, *Lust for Life*

"You may find yourself in a situation where jealousy, anger, or something powerful like hate takes over a person around you. I want you to try to watch them, objectively, observe everything about how they move, the way that they talk. You'll notice that people who act under the impression of intense and extreme emotions are often times unruly. You cannot have a conversation with them, you cannot disagree and have dialogue, everything for them is too intense and they can't even rationalize with you. Don't judge these people, just remember that you cannot forget things you read. After reading this do not forget how out of control they look and appear. Don't be that person. Experience your emotions but learn how to control them so they do not control you..."

—Sylvester McNutt III, *Lust for Life*

"The geniuses of this generation have to figure out how to use one thing better than everyone else: **attention**."

—Sylvester McNutt III, *Lust for Life*

"They always say that any attention is good attention, and I never had an opinion on this until I realized something. If you're trying to become a legend, trying to create a brand, or if you do anything that results in you getting paid, then you need attention. The more people who know about your work, the more people who have an opinion, and the more a person can speak about your work, then the better off you'll be. Good, bad, or indifferent— as long as they are talking about you, you are winning."

—Sylvester McNutt III, *Lust for Life*

"Your desire is to embrace your genius, but the truth is, you live around a bunch of stupid people. Never waste time trying to prove to them that you are gifted. They simply do not operate at the level of consciousness needed to truly grasp and understand what and who you are. You have to do this for yourself, for your legacy, and for your happiness only."

—Sylvester McNutt III, *Lust for Life*

"The culture that you live in has done a lot to break down your perception of self. The majority of the people whom you will come across have been broken—people who have no idea who they are or what they can offer to the world. If you look around, objectively, you see a bunch of adults who never healed from their childhood. You might even feel like an outcast in this society. No matter what you do, don't allow the broken, the jaded, the people who are not winning, to tell you about what you cannot do. You have to reject their negativity, their hate, and their lack of vision. Reject it."

—Sylvester McNutt III, *Lust for Life*

"I'm all for people putting themselves in a situation to win, a situation that works for them. If you have to cut me off, break up with me, or need to go away from me, I will always root for you. My heart is just set up like that; however, I have enough love for myself to only allow people in my life who genuinely want to be around. So if you decide to go, under your own power, please accept that under my power, I have the right to keep you away because I'm not playing musical chairs with my life."

—Sylvester McNutt III, *Lust for Life*

"Refusing to accept that power is a part of life is another form of death. This society will destroy your life if you do not seek to understand power, psychology, sociology, communication, and any other realm of study that helps us understand human behavior. Be obsessed with learning because all we have in life is information, and if you openly reject your pursuit of information, then you are giving your power away. Be aware. Be smart."

—Sylvester McNutt III, *Lust for Life*

"A genius understands that everything can be taken away, especially if something is taken for granted. That's why appreciating what you have before you lose it is vital."

—Sylvester McNutt III, *Lust for Life*

"When people do not have logical responses for what you're saying or your position on something, they may go off the deep end and say the most outrageous things to get a response out of you. Train yourself to never respond to anything immediately, especially things that are rooted nonsense. When you give up control because your emotions were triggered, then you lose in that situation every single time."

—Sylvester McNutt III, *Lust for Life*

"The wise person in the room will never try to act like he or she knows everything, because that is never a wise move. A wise one will always observe and listen to others' perspectives. He or she may be the most correct and the most on point, but a highly conscious being doesn't feel the need to be right. Standing out isn't always the best play, and sometimes you have to just sit back, pause, and collect data without revealing everything that you know."

—Sylvester McNutt III, *Lust for Life*

"When you say things like "I know already," you block yourself from the ability to learn more. A closed mind can never be fed, so instead of rejecting information, be open to it all even if it is something you're familiar with. Even if you have heard another version of what's being presented, observe and absorb it all."

—Sylvester McNutt III, *Lust for Life*

Free Your Genius

I want you to believe, even if it's only for five minutes, that you have a genius inside you. Once you can believe that, then you can enhance your life in any department: financial, spiritual, relationships, happiness, or any other avenues that are important to you.

But step one is to believe in yourself.

Then, step two is to become obsessed with the process of learning and growing.

The final step is to never try to outshine anyone intentionally, but if you do so, allow it to happen in the process of you living inside your purpose and finding your internal flashlight.

—Sylvester McNutt III, *Lust for Life*

10: Lust for Life

"People die every second of every day but how many people are really living? A lot of people are alive but how many of them are really living?

 I hope you do not wait until your time is almost up to decide to lust for life, you should do that now, you should take all those chances and live your life abundantly now."

—Sylvester McNutt III, *Lust for Life*

"You are not working this hard to be broke, to be down, to be unlucky, or to be unruly. You are deserving of love, happiness, and unlimited abundance."

—Sylvester McNutt III, *Lust for Life*

"I used to think that I was broke because the money was hidden and trapped inside the upper class because they were smarter than me, because they were more deserving of it than I was. And then, I started to change my mind-set because I no longer wanted to be at the bottom. I no longer wanted to suffer, to feel like I wasn't good enough.

Once I changed my mind-set on what I deserved, everything changed. Everything grew. Everything started to become fruitful and full of life.

I feel as if this was all about me making the decision first, the decision that I deserved abundance, money, and happiness."

—Sylvester McNutt III, *Lust for Life*

...that's the secret that they don't want you to know about because knowing it will change the entire way that society operates.

The trick is to know that you can achieve just about anything that you are willing to fail at. You can attract and hold financial richness, spiritual richness, and consistent happiness, but it's all about making the choice that you don't deserve anything less than that.

—Sylvester McNutt III, *Lust for Life*

"Working all of the time and having money none of the time is a special kind of hell."

—Sylvester McNutt III, *Lust for Life*

"The majority of people work all of the time and have a budget none of the time. How are you supposed to be financially free if you enslave yourself to poor behaviors like this?

Effective immediately, you need a written budget, and tons of discipline. Don't whine and complain about being broke if you're not on a budget."

—Sylvester McNutt III, *Lust for Life*

"I have a monthly budget. I have a weekly budget. I have a daily budget. Finances are important to me. I am one hundred percent aware of who I owe, if I owe anyone, and I have clear intentions to pay. Debt is slavery and nobody owns me, therefore I refuse to put myself in the negative. If you cannot make these statements above then you need to write a budget and create a plan right now. Being financially free is not only making a million dollars per year, it's having the right behaviors in place so you know how to manage the millions that you will make in your lifetime."

—Sylvester McNutt III, *Lust for Life*

"Open your bank account right now, take a look at it, and tell me what you see. Does it feel like safety or does it give you anxiety. Well, if you're not comfortable with what you see there are only two realistic options that you can do to change that feeling. First, you have to reduce your expenses. Second, you have to increase your income. Third, you must repeat the first two steps over and over until that original emotion changes."

—Sylvester McNutt III, *Lust for Life*

"Growing up, nobody ever talked to me about money, in fact I had religious parents, and they always talked about how a good soul didn't need money. They never saved money. They lived check to check and when an emergency came up we did what we could to get by, but we ultimately dealt with suffering as a result of their mindset. They instilled in me what I like to call **scarcity mindset.** People who believe in the scarcity mindset believe that they are not worthy of financial freedom, they believe that they do not deserve to be rich, and they feel shame when they talk to other people about making money. If you ever want to be financially free you have to get rid of the scarcity mindset immediately. This mindset is the only reason why you're broke, why you're living check to check, and why you're not living the life that you deserve."

—Sylvester McNutt III, *Lust for Life*

"Sit back and listen to music, music that doesn't have any words in it at all— music that feels good to you. Allow your mind to drift, and when you feel yourself floating into a daydream, imagine wealth, imagine happiness, imagine bliss. Imagine every emotion that you want to feel, every thought that may feel good to you. Allow your daydream to take you there."

—Sylvester McNutt III, *Lust for Life*

"It's never about just thinking and hoping about what you want because real success, in any pillar, is always about the work that you put in. I don't want to hear you talking about what you deserve, what you're entitled to, and how you deserve more if you have not put the work in to truly honor such a request. The key to love, to abundance, and to richness is to fully believe that you are deserving of it, without a shadow of doubt. After you believe, then, and only then, are you able to take the actions necessary to earn everything that you're deserving of. This isn't about entitlement; it's about belief, and it's about action."

—Sylvester McNutt III, *Lust for Life*

"I want to feel alive, and that doesn't mean that I just want a heartbeat with flesh that sheds. I want to feel goosebumps down my arm when music hits the right spot. I want to savor every taste of foods that are new. I want to learn new dances that cause me to shake my hips and shoulders in motions that I've never done. I want to watch movies that make me think, movies that make me laugh, and sports that make me yell. I want to love with all my heart, with conviction, and with passion. I don't want to just have a heartbeat; I want to have an unparalleled lust for life."

—Sylvester McNutt III, *Lust for Life*

I don't care anymore about how this outside world is going to judge me; I don't. I have to believe in myself and take these risks because nobody gave me a damn thing. When I fail and take losses, there is nobody there to pick me up. If I go broke, there will be no handouts. If I feel depressed, no one will tell me to cheer up. It's all up to me, and it's been that way for a long time. That's why I give everything that I have. That's why I dedicate myself to learning, to living, and to feeling alive. I don't have a plan B; all I have is plan 'now'.

—Sylvester McNutt III, *Lust for Life*

"Nobody will ever have your back in life more than you will have your own back. Save yourself first."

– Sylvester McNutt III, *Lust For Life*

"A real friend is not going to put you in situations that take you past your boundaries, so when they do, you must question that friendship."

– Sylvester McNutt III, *Lust For Life*

"Friends grow apart. It's tough to deal with because the connection used to be so easy to manage. Life changes, just like the current in the oceans. When the connection starts to fade you can try to keep it but never force it. Life is telling you to grow, so grow, and appreciate everything that you brought each other."

– Sylvester McNutt III, *Lust For Life*

"I think about the lovers who didn't want to take a risk with me, the ones who couldn't forgive me for my flaws, the ones who couldn't commit because I wasn't wild enough, the ones who wouldn't give me a chance because I wasn't mature enough. I think about the ones who stayed for a minute, only to be gone the next hour. I think about how I was beatdown and broken, but I gave every ounce of my love away because I wanted others to feel it, no matter how weak I was. I knew that love had the power to give strength. It's all I knew. I think about how they didn't stay, how they weren't ready, and how they'll always think about me even though they love someone else now. I'll never leave their hearts or their minds; my love doesn't go away, even after I do."

—Sylvester McNutt III, *Lust for Life*

"I just experienced the most moving nostalgia that my heart has ever registered. I looked back on a broken situation that I healed. I looked back on the broken person that I was, and I shed one tear, because I healed and turned into the person that I always knew I could be. I looked back because I can see that I am moving forward, and well, the only thing better than winning is winning after you have taken a bunch of losses."

—Sylvester McNutt III, *Lust for Life*

"It's life, you will experience some losses, but as long as you keep learning you'll eventually start winning. With every loss never worry about the loss, instead, focus on the lessons that you take so you can be better the next time around."

—Sylvester McNutt III, *Lust for Life*

"You really have to be proud of yourself. You've overcome obstacles that others died from. You bounced back when you should've been too broken to breathe. You healed these scars that would've disabled others. You're as strong as the winds of a hurricane, your fight when you're supposed to quit, and you shine when the world wants to dim your light. Be proud of everything that you've overcome."

—Sylvester McNutt III, *Lust for Life*

"The great thing about feeling broken is accepting that it can't get any worse. Once you realize that you're at the bottom the only logical place you can go from there is towards the top."

—Sylvester McNutt III, *Lust for Life*

"If you're going through a tough you have to employ patience, but you have to be extremely proactive with your goals. The only way you'll get out is if you set realistic goals and take one step towards that goal everyday. A house gets built by laying brick after brick, your story is not different from that house. Be patient and lay a brick every single day until your foundation is solid, until you're able to rewire yourself, until you're able to happily put new tenants in the home."

—Sylvester McNutt III, *Lust for Life*

"A lot of people want to escape Sunday nights so that they don't have to wake up on Monday. They're tired of going to the job that is unfulfilling while living check to check and suffering through the grind in what feels like a rat race. I suppose making money is important especially since we live in a world that requires money to obtain resources; however, nothing is more important than happiness and mental health. If the job is causing depression, a deep feeling of regret, and there is a lack of fulfillment, I feel the only alternative is to seek other options. Why not be happy in a job that is enjoyable?"

—Sylvester McNutt III, *Lust for Life*

"If you want to build a business, a brand, or there's a product you're looking to create, you should go for it. However, you don't have to quit your job and dive all the way in, right away. Some people give you the advice that you should quit your job right away, and I'm telling you the truth: if you do that, you will enter desperation mode. Use the job to fund your business, keep the benefits, and take your time building your own building."

—Sylvester McNutt III, *Lust for Life*

Think about it like this. If you drive by a car that has its hood down and if the driver is sitting in the car, you would never pull over and stop to help. You're not even sure if he or she really needs help because the person is just pulled over on the side of the road and is not proactively telling the universe that he or she is deserving of help. If you drove by a car and you saw someone fixing a tire, or under the hood, or trying to get attention to get help, the odds of you stopping are drastically higher. Why? Because it's much easier to help someone who is already helping himself or herself. This applies from every angle. If you are the helper, be mindful of how much energy you're investing because it is his or her responsibility to take care of his or her life. You can't do the work for him or her, and your main goal should be to assist him or her in the parts that he or she is struggling with, not to do the whole thing. If you're the person who needs help, don't take advantage of the help to the point where the helper feels used and underappreciated, but do everything in your power to take advantage of the help by helping yourself as much as you can so that the helper can eventually leave you.

"This generation is obsessed with proving who they are or what they have to strangers online. It's madness. Intimate details and happenings in someone's life do not need to be on the Internet for them to be real. Some love sharing, and others do not, but nobody should be pressured or forced to share anything because of their friends or lovers. Everyone has a right to privacy and protection."

—Sylvester McNutt III, *Lust for Life*

"I believe in privacy before I believe in creating a fake image of myself for social media. I keep my personal life private, or as private as I feel, and I only share when I feel inclined to. I do not feel as If I need to put every aspect of my life on social media. It's my business, not yours."

—Sylvester McNutt III, *Lust for Life*

"You can't call me fake because you don't see the real side of me. You watch through social media, so watch, and stay in your lane. The people who are really involved in my life know what's going on."

—Sylvester McNutt III, *Lust for Life*

"Use social media to connect with other human beings who have similar interests. Use it to spread positive messages. Use social media to find interesting events in your area. Use social media to add value to other people's lives by sharing information that you're passionate about. Social media is a great tool, we owe it to ourselves to use it right."

—Sylvester McNutt III, *Lust for Life*

I've meet some great people through social media: business partners, friendships that will last forever, and even another human who feels like real love. Never ever say, "it's just social media". It's much bigger than that. It's literally a path to connect to other human beings.

—Sylvester McNutt III, *Lust for Life*

"You should be living free, totally free of suffering, totally lusting for life. If you're not, look closely at your life, take an inventory of what needs to stay, and destroy everything else that needs to go."

—Sylvester McNutt III, *Lust for Life*

"You need to book a ticket to go to a new place right now to expand your view of the world. You need to go to a new city this month to learn about a culture that is outside of your own, even if it's a city in the next state. You need to try new foods, foods that have history, culture, and a robust flavor that you have never tasted. You need to take a different route home from work and stop at a random restaurant or museum. Break the routine, step outside of your comfort zone, and feel something different."

—Sylvester McNutt III, *Lust for Life*

"You work too hard; you give too much to not see everything that this world has to offer. It is time that you fulfill that itch that has been bothering you. Get out in the world, get out of your own way, and travel."

—Sylvester McNutt III

"Your daily motivation should be the fact that every day that goes by equates to one day closer to your death. This should shock you. This thought, this realization, this raw truth should motivate you. How much more time do you have? How many more opportunities are you going to let go? How many more times are you going to box yourself in? Life is such a precious, rewarding, and interesting journey, but if you don't become obsessed with learning and growing, you will suffer. You will live with a nagging regret that will never go away if you don't take charge. Once you read something like this, you can never go back to your normal life; you simply can't. We must both ask and answer this question for ourselves, every day: If I only had six more months to live, would I feel like I have accomplished everything that I wanted to do?"

—Sylvester McNutt III, *Lust for Life*

Don't take out loans that you don't need.
Don't borrow things from people if you're
able to earn them yourself. Owing favors
and debt is just another form of slavery,
and you're allowing people to control you if
you owe anyone anything. Don't borrow.
Don't let people control you.

—Sylvester McNutt III, *Lust for Life*

"You have to get out of debt. Debt is killing your happiness. Living check to check is not fun, and you don't deserve that anymore. Start by creating a monthly budget. The monthly budget will help you develop the behaviors needed to hold your money. Declutter your house, and get rid of all your stuff; once you do that, stop buying stuff just for the sake of buying them. If a thing doesn't serve a functional purpose, don't buy it. If it's not in your budget, don't buy it. Get out of debt, and give yourself that mental freedom that you deserve; otherwise the debt will control you, and you no longer deserve that."

—Sylvester McNutt III, *Lust for Life*

"I don't want anyone to own me, to control me, or to box me into his or her perspectives of what I should be. It doesn't work like that for me. I will say no to help that comes with conditions. I will say hell no to people who want to control my mind and box me in."

—Sylvester McNutt III, *Lust for Life*

Quitting Your Job to Become an Entrepreneur?

Quitting your job isn't always the path to follow if you desire to be an entrepreneur or if you feel like you're not genuinely satisfied with your current job. The best advice I can give you is to build your side hustle while you're in your job. You have to think big picture about this. You are ready to quit your job now because you don't feel fulfilled. You're ready to quit now because you've burned out in a sense.

Entrepreneurship is going to require ten times the effort you've been giving. Entrepreneurs are always tired, always need to recharge, and we may not show it, but we operate with fear. A true entrepreneur knows that he or she can lose everything in the blink of an eye—that's scary, and motivating. We don't get to sleep in. We don't get to make as many mistakes that you can make at a job. At the job, you get written up, and you just have to stick to the policy. As an entrepreneur, you might lose a $1,000 customer or sale because you missed one little detail, and you have to be ready to deal with that type of defeat.

Your title and expectations at the job hardly change, but when you become an entrepreneur, you are the CEO, the marketing, facilities, training, sales, Internet marketing, customer service, and product creation all in one. If you have been working a job for a certain amount of time, don't quit to chase your dreams. Your dreams might not pay you. Figure out what you're good at and what you're terrible at. You need a high level of self-awareness first before you try to spend one day as a full-time entrepreneur. On the other hand, you may just need a different job.

Give everything that you have to your job, learn everything that you can, and go home every night with a vigor to focus on your craft. Build up your side job, your product, or your business as much as you can, and when the universe tells you to go all in, jump, and don't look back. If you know that you're going to quit your job, stop partying, stop drinking, and stop celebrating. The only thing you need to do is focus on saving money and getting rid of all your expenses. Sell all your stuff, don't buy anything new, and be ready to be broke until you get over the hump. I write this to you not as a theory, not as an idea, but as a person who did it word for word. I wish you nothing but peace, love, and joy on your journey of entrepreneurship or to find the job that suits you best. You spend 30 percent of your life working so you might as well enjoy it.

Healing after a Bad Breakup

We all know that relationships have the ability to rip us apart and leave us lying there without a clue on how to put ourselves back together. I don't want to give you a one-liner that just says, "Move on." I want to give you something real, something deep, and something that hopefully gives you a realistic ray of hope.

First, I am speaking to you as a person who has had to recover from what you're going through right now. I want you to know that you are not alone in your feelings. You may feel weak, you may feel like nobody can love you the way he or she did, or you may feel as if you wasted valuable years of your life because now that person is no longer in your life.

You are correct. You are right, and you have every right to be upset about feeling like you had your time wasted, but hear me out. When I was in your position, I determined that I deserved to feel real love, that I didn't deserve to cry myself to sleep, and that this person was a lesson to me. A tough lesson, but nonetheless, it was a lesson. Every single day I told myself these words: "You will overcome," and "You are a being of love." I still say these words now, and I'm not dealing with any pain. I got into the habit of saying this because I wanted to heal, and these simple phrases did so much for me. I challenge you to simply say it aloud right now with an open mind; see how that feels. You'll see that it actually gives you a sense of closure and hope. These words give you power to take charge and to move forward. You will overcome; you are a being of love.

"You will overcome this tough moment because your heart is designed to bounce back and to prosper. You are a being of love and beings with your kind of energy cannot stay down for too long. Roll with the punches so life doesn't knock you out and then throw your own punch back at life, that's called a counter punch."

—Sylvester McNutt III, *Lust for Life*

"At the very least, love yourself. At the very least, do everything that you can to make sure that your life is enjoyable."

—Sylvester McNutt III, *Lust for Life*

"Call off of work today. You need a self-care day: eat good, rest, cleanse, meditate, and do activities that lift up your energy. You are deserving of this."

—Sylvester McNutt III, *Lust for Life*

"I am crazy, but it won't kill me. They tell me that I work too much, but I'm not going to stop grinding. They tell me that I dream too big, but I won't stop shooting for the moon. I believe in me the same way you believe that the sun will come up after the night. Nobody, and I mean nobody, is allowed to dictate my success or the level of effort that I am willing to put out to manifest my dreams. I will not allow my friends, my family, my lover, or myself to tell me what I cannot do. And if they step on the toes of me getting to my dreams, then they might get their feet cut off. I am obsessed, and it's because I know what I deserve. I am not willing to settle, to give up, or to lose. I am worthy of success, I am worthy of abundance, and I am worthy of happiness. I will rest when I die, and when I come back in my next human body, I will multiply my effort to the next level. This energy cannot be destroyed."

—Sylvester McNutt III, *Lust for Life*

"People always make it seem like you need a plan. I agree to the extent that a plan can help you stay focused, can gear you toward the most efficient path for your goals, and can ensure that you stay the course. However, more important than a plan is the right energy. Energy will always outweigh a plan in my eyes. If you eat like crap, keep negative people around you, and don't cleanse your body of the spiritual and physical toxins that you absorb, you will simply die. I hate to be so blunt, but I have to be real and honest. I had the opportunity to observe people whom I loved kill themselves because they refused to distance themselves from negative people, substances, and foods. Nothing is more important than energy; you literally are a being of energy. You do not need a plan to be successful, but you need the correct energy."

—Sylvester McNutt III, *Lust for Life*

A Letter to My Soul Mate:

I do care about you, about love, and about family. I also care that we commit to our connection over everything. If we can commit to working internally to grow, if we can commit to communicating consistently, and if we can commit to choosing to prioritize our connection over it all, then I don't feel like we will lose. A lot of great parents prioritize their kids over their relationship with their spouses, and nobody will ever fault them for putting their children first. But I hope that we can learn to show our children the value in valuing our connection to each other. I want them to see us love, care for, and speak to each other with kindness and compassion because I feel that is a value that they should have. I don't want to lose you because I stopped paying attention to you. I don't want you to lose me because you forgot to love me. I need you; I want you. I want to keep reinventing our love over and over, and I want our kids to know that they might need to go to bed earlier because Mommy and Daddy need some love time.

—Sylvester McNutt III, *Lust for Life*

This Is What's Missing from Today's Relationships

I got up off the couch, a place I had been sitting for the last twenty-seven minutes, half-reading poetry and half-watching *Beetlejuice*. She had been in the kitchen for the last hour, making chicken breast, salad, and homemade dressings. I felt a genuine loneliness even though she wasn't away but nearby. I took one sip of my wine from the table and started walking toward her. I said, "Babe, I know that you're cooking, but I really need you to serve the food, even if it's not all done. One, I'm really hungry, and two, I'm really lonely with you being in here." She smiled, look at me angelically, and asked, "After we eat, can you come back into the kitchen so I can put the dishes away?" "Of course." I smiled. Our generation is missing this. It's missing the desire for each of us to really care and value human connection. It's something we need, and I know those cell phones have important features, but let's learn to put them down and to replace them with each other. Let's remember to prioritize our relationships and the effort that we put into them.

—Sylvester McNutt III, *Lust for Life*

This Is What's Missing from Today's Relationships

How about after work one day you both go home, turn your phones off, and talk about everything other than work. Turn on ambient music that has no words but an immaculate sound. Pull out a deck of cards or a journal and simply sit there with each other with only one intention, the one intention of being connected to each other through activity, through conversation, and through bonding like we are supposed to do. Today's relationships are missing this component because it's so easy for us to get on our phones and laptops when we get home. It's so easy for us to throw on Netflix and forget to engage with each other. It's easy for us to forget how important it is to do simple things like engage, talk, and look at each other. If you have a relationship or are trying to build one, never forget this; never forget how valuable it is to invest time and energy into your relationships.

—Sylvester McNutt III, *Lust for Life*

"Never give up on your dreams because everyone else gave up on theirs. Never talk down to yourself because others do. Never settle for minimum effort from yourself when you should be giving your maximum."

—Sylvester McNutt III, *Lust for Life*

I woke up today and realized that it was OK for me to walk away from everything and everyone who brought me consistent pain, especially if I tried to communicate that position. I accept that I deserve bliss, happiness, and a consistent state of love. Anything else will not be accepted.

—Sylvester McNutt III, *Lust for Life*

The goal is to lust for life.
The goal is to live free;
the goal is to feel bold.
The goal is to chase
happiness and peace.

—Sylvester McNutt III, *Lust for Life*

Lust for Life: a person who wants to experience all the joys of life, especially the ones that society has told him or her that he or she does not deserve, a person who wants to feel total bliss and abundance of happiness and love. A person who is lusting for life genuinely wants the people he or she knows to let go of the pain and discomfort they feel and to accept that there is nothing but love, financial freedom, peace, and internal harmony available for them to access.

—Sylvester McNutt III, *Lust for Life*

"I will not wait for anyone to give me permission to live my life, to go after what I want, or to be the person that I want to be. My desire is to *lust for life*, to live ego-free, and to attract everything that I deserve. I will not make apologies to anyone for being myself. I love myself. I want to love my friends and family members too, however, everyone must meet me at this level. I have no more energy left to live in a vibration that doesn't feel good. I cannot feel sad or depressed. I only want joy, happiness, and love for me and for you - come with me."

—Sylvester McNutt III, *Lust for Life*

Thank you for reading my sixth book, Lust For Life. I am nothing without you, but I am everything with you. I wanted this book to inspire you to break old habits while trying new activities. If you ever get lost in the world go find *Lust For Life* and it will be there to put you not he right path. I am an independent author, free of a company owning my creative control, but I am dependent upon my true fans. I need you to leave a positive five-star review on **amazon.com** and any other source where people review books. A five-star review gives me more movement to keep inspiring people through writing. It helps me to continue to feed my family. If you feel like I've earned a five star ranking, please leave it. Share this energy with someone you love,

Keep Loving, Keep Living.

Sylvester McNutt III
Sep 13th, 2017

Made in the USA
San Bernardino, CA
24 June 2020

74097753R00224